# Praise for
# The Power to Persist

"If there's one book you read cover to cover this year, let it be *The Power to Persist*."

—**Michelle Miller,** award-winning journalist; *New York Times* best-selling author; co-host, *CBS Saturday Morning*

"*The Power to Persist* is an inspiring and exciting read, which I strongly recommend to anyone who is seeking to elevate their skills and achieve positive results in the face of adversity."

—**Adam Silver,** NBA commissioner

"*The Power to Persist* is a road map for anyone looking to overcome obstacles and elevate their personal lives or careers. Lamell uses a mix of his own inspiring stories and tried-and-true methods to help readers confront adversity and reach their full potential."

—**David Kohler,** chair and CEO, Kohler Co.

"Stocked full of practical tips for self-improvement, *The Power to Persist* is this year's best book in personal growth."

—**Randall Woodfin,** mayor of Birmingham

"If you're looking for a way to optimize your life, *The Power to Persist* is for you."

—**Jordyn O. Hudson,** documentary filmmaker; founder, CircleBlaq; Harvard Graduate School of Education

"As an educator and public servant, I've spent my life helping others navigate challenges and realize their potential. *The Power to Persist* is a compelling and practical guide that does just that—equipping readers with the mindset and tools to thrive through adversity."

—**Dr. Larry Rice,** former university president; chief engagement officer, Northern Compass Consulting

"*The Power to Persist* teaches you how to unlock the superpowers of resilience in a down-to-earth and relatable fashion."

—**Marc H. Morial,** president and CEO, National Urban League

"Mindset matters! In *The Power to Persist*, Lamell McMorris walks you through how to change your mindset to achieve powerful and meaningful results. His teachings take you from 'I can't' to 'I can.'"

—**Dr. J. D. LaRock,** president and CEO, Network for Teaching Entrepreneurship (NFTE)

"This well-written, timely book is great for readers at any stage of life. Whether you're on the threshold of a new career or a seasoned veteran, you'll find motivation in McMorris's advice and encouragement to bring your best to all you wish to accomplish."

—**John Hudson,** senior vice president and chief external affairs officer; president, Entergy Charitable Foundation

"The journey to success is filled with setbacks, but *The Power to Persist* is filled with smart and manageable ways to transform them into setups for success."

—**Timothy Murphy,** vice chair, Mastercard

# THE
# POWER
## TO
# PERSIST

8 Simple Habits to Build
LIFELONG RESILIENCE

## Lamell J. McMorris

**FAST**
**COMPANY**
*Press*

Fast Company Press
New York, New York
www.fastcompanypress.com

This work is being published under the Fast Company Press imprint by an
exclusive arrangement with *Fast Company*. *Fast Company* and the *Fast
Company* logo are registered trademarks of Mansueto Ventures, LLC.
The Fast Company Press logo is a wholly owned trademark of Mansueto
Ventures, LLC.

Distributed by Greenleaf Book Group

For ordering information or special discounts for bulk purchases, please
contact Greenleaf Book Group at PO Box 91869, Austin, TX  78709,
512.891.6100.

Design and composition by Greenleaf Book Group and Jonathan Lewis
Cover design by Greenleaf Book Group and Jonathan Lewis
Cover images used under license from ©Adobestock.com/jules
The Power to Persist Framework Octagon on page 10 by
Vertical Marketr LLC

Publisher's Cataloging-in-Publication data is available.

Print ISBN: 978-1-63908-143-1

eBook ISBN: 978-1-63908-144-8

To offset the number of trees consumed in the printing of our books,
Greenleaf donates a portion of the proceeds from each printing to the
Arbor Day Foundation. Greenleaf Book Group has replaced over 50,000
trees since 2007.

Printed in the United States of America on acid-free paper

25  26  27  28  29  30  31     10  9  8  7  6  5  4  3  2  1

First Edition

To my mom, whose unwavering
resilience and strength inspire me every day.

This book is a tribute to your incredible spirit
and the lessons you've taught me about perseverance.

# CONTENTS

# Foreword

by REVEREND AL SHARPTON

Resilience has played a tremendous role in my life. I was born and raised in Brooklyn, New York—my parents owned a corner store and some real estate. We eventually moved out to a middle-class Black neighborhood in Queens, and I became a boy preacher in the Pentecostal church. One day, I woke up—I was ten years old—and my mother told my sister and me that our father had left—he had run off with my mother's daughter from her previous marriage and abandoned us. That absolutely crushed me.

So, we moved back to Brooklyn, but this time in the housing projects. I had never known what the housing projects were because we were middle class in Queens. And now we had to buy our groceries with food stamps. But every morning, my mother would take the subway to downtown Manhattan to scrub floors as a domestic worker. She sacrificed herself to feed her family and subsidize us with welfare. I would walk her to the station, and she told me, "Don't worry. Life is not about where you start. Life's about where you are going."

I never heard her complain about losing our middle-class house in Queens. I never heard her complain about what Daddy did. She showed me what resilience is. As I got into my own career, and I fought civil rights cases and faced all sorts of controversies and attacks, I was already trained by my mother to just keep bouncing back.

We all face things in life that can knock the legs out from under us. And you've got to believe you can get back up—you've got to believe that the knockdowns only make you stronger.

That's also the case for my good friend Lamell McMorris. I first met Lamell when he was a traveling assistant to Reverend Jesse Jackson. I had been a mentee of Reverend Jackson for many years. When I was twelve years old, I joined Operation Breadbasket—I was already a boy preacher—and when I was thirteen, Reverend Jackson appointed me as the youth director of the New York chapter. So I've seen a lot of people come and go.

When I first saw Lamell with Reverend Jackson in the late nineties, there was just something about him that seemed unique and different because he was driven to achieve and make a difference. I've seen a lot of people come and go around Reverend Jackson, and later, I would see a lot of people come and go around me as I developed my own national leadership. I'm always looking for people who have a special kind of commitment and a special kind of what we call the "Black church anointing." I could instantly see that Lamell had that, and he still does today.

Lamell was with Coretta Scott King, Martin Luther King III, and me when we did the commemorative March on Washington in 2000—he was the executive director of SCLC at the time. Twenty-four years later, we still do it and draw between 150,000 and 200,000 people.

I've seen Lamell go through ups and downs in his career and in business, but he never changed his faith, never seemed to waver. Today, he's on the board of my organization, the National Action Network, and he's still that activist, still that true-believing-at-heart lay clergyman I met when he was much younger in the nineties. He has not lost that commitment. You meet a lot of people in movements such as civil rights, but you don't meet a lot of people that you know in their heart—their core heart—they believe that people can rise. Lamell is one of those people who believes.

You can take your advice from people who have theoretical knowledge about a topic, but it's something else to take advice from someone who has had their own challenges and who can share their experiences. In this book, that's what Lamell has delivered. Mike Tyson, who I knew well, used to say, "Everybody's got a plan until they get punched in the face." Lamell has put the advice in this book into practice. He's been punched a few times—he's been knocked down, he's been discarded, he's been marginalized—but every time, he still found a way to bounce back and win the fight.

There's no one I know who has achieved more in their life when the odds were against them than Lamell. He didn't inherit anything—he fought for everything he achieved and was trained and mentored by some of the greatest figures of his community in his time. There's no one who has that unique kind of education. The other guys went to Morehouse, but they didn't grow up in the house of those people who shaped the domestic agenda of the most powerful nation in the world. Lamell has that unique background.

He didn't study it in school; he lived it in life. And I know you will benefit greatly from what you're about to read.

**—Rev. Al Sharpton,** New York City

# On the Road to Resilience

Resilience is not just some crazy idea or feel-good concept I've latched onto; it's been my constant companion for as long as I can remember. I've had to be resilient from the start of my life until now, and I'm certain that I'm going to be close friends with resilience until the day I breathe my last breath.

My name is Lamell McMorris, and I was born and grew up in a very rough part of Chicago. While I have enjoyed more than my share of success over the years, it didn't start out that way.

I never met my biological father—the only thing I know is that he owned a business, and he was killed in a robbery. I've never even seen a picture of him, and as far as I know, I've never interacted with anyone in his family. My mom married Henry McMorris when I was in third grade, and he adopted me; up until that point, my name was Lamell Hunter.

As a latchkey kid, born to a single mom who worked multiple jobs and with a brother twelve years older than me, I was almost always left on my own to cook and entertain myself. When I was growing up, I literally had to dodge bullets from drug and gang violence (not to mention somehow avoid not getting recruited into a gang) as I walked to school or just went outside to play or hang out with my friends around our apartment at 66th and Cottage Grove in the notorious west side of Woodlawn. We lived just steps away from Parkway Gardens (check out the history of "O Block"), sandwiched between Cottage Grove and King Drive.

There's a book titled *Black Gangsters of Chicago* that details the transition of my neighborhood from affluence to poverty:

> Before World War II, the thriving commercial activity of Woodlawn's Sixty-third and Cottage Avenue was rivaled only by State Street in the Loop. Woodlawn hopped as a center for blues music, and dozens of bars, clubs, and ballrooms stretched from Cottage Grove to Stoney Island. But when the U.S. Supreme Court made the infamous restrictive covenants unenforceable in 1948, Woodlawn's character and racial makeup changed. Poor black Southerners poured into Chicago. By the mid-1950s, the white flight from Woodlawn was well underway.[1]

By the time I was born, Woodlawn was just a faint shadow of its former vibrant self. As *Black Gangsters of Chicago* describes the scene, "Landlords vacated buildings. The income level dropped. Families crowded into substandard housing. And the crime rate soared. Woodlawn sank into poverty."[2] Thousands of boys and men joined gangs, most notably the Blackstone Rangers. According to an article in *The Atlantic*, members of this gang had "been charged with murder, robbery, rape, knifings, extortion of South Side merchants, traffic in narcotics, extortion and intimidation of young children, forced gang membership, and a general history of outright violence."[3]

Believe me, when I tell people who really know Chicago neighborhoods where I'm from, they almost always do a double take. Bertha and Henry ultimately divorced as I entered high school at Whitney Young. My thirst for student government and advocacy grew, and I found a new hero in Harold Washington, the first Black mayor of Chicago.

I had a double-barrel shotgun pointed at my chest during a robbery in Atlanta as a sophomore at Morehouse College. I faced getting kicked out of Morehouse every semester I was there because I didn't have the money for tuition. I had to literally sit in the VP of Finance's office and dial for dollars while being locked out of registration and running around begging teachers to add me to their classes. Yet I still graduated on time, and an oil painting of me hangs in Morehouse today, along with other luminaries and accomplished alumni.

Today, I lead the Washington, D.C.–based consulting firm, Phase 2 Consulting, which is one of D.C.'s top strategic advisory firms, providing expertise for government affairs, corporate social responsibility planning, and public policy advice. Before that, I was in charge of the Regulatory and Government Relations practice for Edward Jones. In addition, I currently serve as trustee and chair for the National Urban League's committee on governance, and I sit on the National Action Network's executive committee. I'm a board member for the Rainbow/PUSH coalition and serve on the board of trustees for PGA REACH.

I am blessed to have had the opportunity to accomplish a lot in my relatively short time on earth. But I've also been fired multiple times, had businesses shuttered, faced insurmountable debt—tax liens, bill collectors, and all the rest—and I've been on the brink of losing it all. Despite all that, I have constantly kept the face of prosperity, success, joy, and progress as the prevailing narrative in my life. I embraced this duality, this double consciousness, of living in your purpose and pushing forward in spite of the odds, even while the ground beneath you is sinking and your life is far from what others may think.

Successful businessman. OK, if you say so. Committed and passionate advocate and leader in civil and social justice. Yup, that too. Devoted friend and loyal ally and mentor. Without a doubt. But failed, struggling, stressed, and lack of sleep are my middle names and claims to fame as well. Throughout all the ups and downs, I have made it my life's mission to lift others up and help *them* build their own stock of resilience—to demonstrate that someone sees them and cares.

Let me give you an example.

It's not unusual for me to try to connect something meaningful to my birthday. I look at birthdays as a golden opportunity for resets, realignment, confirmation but also affirmation about who we are and who we aspire to be. And so, I always try to do something positive on my birthday—to party with a purpose, if you will.

This year, however, I raised the bar even higher, pursuing Twenty-Two Days of Gratitude in the weeks leading up to my birthday. My idea was to model behavior around gratitude and give back to some folks around the country who had faced hard times and could use a helping hand—to know that someone cared. And instead of simply making my contributions from afar, I made a personal commitment to actually visit the people I planned to help, making the kind of human connection that writing a check or sending some cash via Venmo just can't accomplish.

I also wanted to show that helping people doesn't always mean you have to do something big and monumental—you don't have to find a cure for cancer, you don't have to build a new school, and you don't have to buy someone a new house or car. There is an almost endless variety of small, simple things you can do that have the power to make a big difference in people's lives.

So, with making a personal connection with each of these people locked in, the challenge for me was to figure out how to weave the Twenty-Two Days of Gratitude into my existing work travel schedule, which had stops all across the country. I quickly figured out that I could make this task much easier by leveraging the many personal, business, and philanthropic relationships I already had with people in most every big city and state.

To kick things off, I started calling the people in my network, explaining how I wanted their help finding some deserving people to reach out to during my Twenty-Two Days of Gratitude. I then asked if they knew someone in their area they would recommend. "Do you know someone in the Phoenix area who needs help?" I asked. Or "I'm going to be in Atlanta—do you know anyone in the area who needs help?" Literally, that's how it all got started.

To be honest, I was more than a little nervous that trying to find twenty-two different people and get everything lined up in time would be completely overwhelming. How in the world was I going to get this done in this very constrained schedule? But when you set the bar high, I believe you encourage yourself to work harder, try harder—thus ensuring your ultimate success. As French soccer star Kylian Mbappé put it, "We must always set the bar high, otherwise we do not progress."

In fact, I filled every one of those twenty-two days with people who needed a helping hand. I'll admit that some of those days didn't fall into place until the last minute, and I wasn't sure I would always have someone to reach out to, but

I believe God made sure I didn't have a single empty day on my calendar.

On Day Eight, I had the privilege of meeting Ms. White, a remarkable, eighty-five-year-young woman in Atlanta who takes care of her hearing-impaired son and desperately needed some groceries. I gave her a call and asked, "What would you like me to bring—what do you need?" As I made a list of the groceries she needed, Ms. White immediately told me about a neighbor down the street whose situation was even worse than her own. The woman was homebound—she couldn't get out of her house at all—*and* she needed some groceries too. Ms. White asked me if it would be all right for her to share some of the groceries I was going to bring her with this neighbor of hers.

All right? I was so inspired by Ms. White's kindness and selflessness that I doubled down at the grocery store, buying even more so she could share them with her neighbor down the street. What was remarkable to me was that she created a ripple effect in her community by telling me about someone else *she* could help—while she needed help herself. Her willingness to think beyond her own situation was both compassionate and generous, and it is a beautiful example for us all to try to emulate in our own lives.

I have long known that giving is contagious, but this generous woman in Atlanta just reinforced the point for me. When you help someone in need, you trigger a ripple across the pond as they think about other people who *they* can help.

I always tell people that everyone thinks that when God speaks, the earth has to start shaking, and a celestial choir has to start singing, and the clouds have to part. But that's not the case at all. If you're paying attention, and I hope you are, God gives us confirmation every day that we're on the right path doing exactly what we're supposed to be doing at this time and place. About a week after I completed my Twenty-Two Days of Gratitude, I was on the treadmill one morning listening to a collection of positive songs, sayings, and affirmations that my friend Latrice Spann had curated and put together for me on Spotify.

And right in the middle of the collection, some guy interrupted the affirmation I was listening to and started talking about gratitude. At first, I thought it was a commercial—I figured that after thirty seconds it would go back to the affirmation I had been listening to. But to my surprise, it kept going. As it turned out, the interruption was a podcast about gratitude, and the host said these words: "Gratitude leads to resilience."

I was like, "My God, where in the world did this come from?" It was almost scary—it came out of nowhere. But as I listened, I found myself entranced by the message that gratitude leads to resilience. It was just another confirmation that having this attitude of gratitude is absolutely a positive step in building resilience.

Imagine that you're a living, breathing battery, and the energy in your battery is constantly being recharged or depleted. Think about the times when you have a tough day at work, or you argue with a spouse or a friend, or things just don't go your way. During times like these, your battery is being depleted, and your resilience is drained—it's harder to get back on your feet when you're knocked down to the ground.

But then think about the times when you achieve an important goal at work or enjoy a nice lunch with your spouse or friend or when everything is going your way. That's when your battery is being recharged and you're building resilience— you're able to bounce right back when times get tough. And the more you recharge that battery, the greater the depth of your resilience.

The podcast reminded me that gratitude is one of the best ways we can build a tremendous well of resilience. The more gratitude we express—especially to those around us through acts of kindness, but even to ourselves—the deeper that well will be and the more we can rely on it when we need it the most. I gained a tremendous amount of energy during the course of my Twenty-Two Days of Gratitude, both from the doing and from seeing how others' lives were impacted—not just those people who received but also those who observed what I did. The feedback was incredible.

But we're not just building resilience in ourselves; we're building resilience in the people we reach out to. I am convinced that the gratitude I expressed to Ms. White boosted her own resilience. She is filled with more hope after our experience because she knows that someone really does care about her. And not just anyone, but someone she hadn't met until that very moment when I showed up in her life. My simple act of kindness made her stronger and better able to bounce back from the inevitable trials and tribulations that await her on life's long journey. This becomes a ripple as people follow my example and do the same in their communities.

Having an attitude of gratitude is just one of the habits in your personal resilience code, and my goal in writing this book is to present you with a proven set of practical tools and habits you can put to work on becoming more resilient in your personal, career, and business life starting today—right *now*.

I want you to learn from personal experience that resilience is not just some notion that sits on a shelf waiting for you to throw out there when you need it. There are habits you must learn, things you must do and *can* do. Some of these things you're already doing. Some are within your current realm, and some you just need to increase. But there are real, concrete steps you can take to develop habits around resilience and become a more resilient person in the face of trials and tribulations—and also opportunities, victories, and success. Because sometimes even with victories and success, you need resilience to hold up to the constant pressure to achieve more, to be more.

Resilience cuts across the line. It's not just about losing; it's also about winning. And this book will show you—in clear and simple terms—how to use some simple but powerful resilience habits to deal with both and always come out ahead.

I look forward to our journey together on the road to resilience.

# The Power to Persist Framework

The 8 habits that fuel resilience, illustrated in the octagon,
serve as the foundation for everything you'll explore in this book.

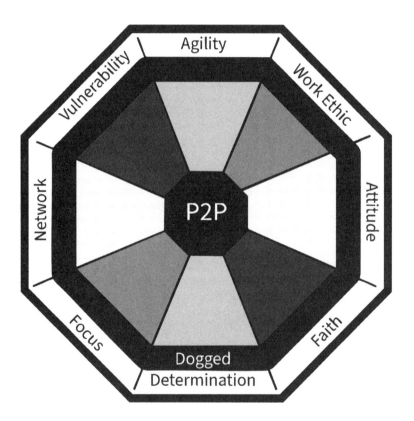

## CHAPTER 1

# A Code for Resilience

**W**elcome to *The Power to Persist*. Maybe you've picked this book up because you're at a crossroads, thinking about how to fortify yourself for the challenges, changes, or new adventures that lie ahead. Maybe you picked it up because you're in a crisis in your career or relationship and are trying to figure out how to cope and gain some sense of control over the outcome. Or maybe you're on cruise control and you want to level up, or you're out there crushing it and just want to learn more.

Whatever brought you to this book, I'm so glad you're here, and I look forward to our journey together to learn about how to cultivate, build, and apply resilience in your day-to-day life.

We can all think of a story of a public figure who used resilience to control an outcome—a star athlete who pushed through an injury for a title-winning game, an entrepreneur who against all odds brought a game-changing product to market and reaped incredible rewards, an entertainer who came from nothing and went on to become a global superstar. These stories all show degrees of remarkable resilience and grit, but sometimes to the rest of us, they can feel really far away and unattainable. It's easy to point to those remarkable stories of success because we rarely hear about the failures that remain anonymous and out of view.

My hope in this book is to speak to the successes *and* the failures that are indeed a lifelong journey, building our muscle of resilience as we go, because while it has a beginning, there truly is no end. Resilience will guide you when you get it right and also when you get it wrong. It will guide you when you're seeking new ideas and challenges or when you're pushing through the mundane. It will come into play in every aspect of your life—from your personal relationships to your career, your health, and your happiness. Through the exercises and guiding principles laid out in this book, you will learn to incorporate the resilience into every aspect of your life to make it more manageable, allowing you to spend more time enjoying it and less time worrying about it.

There are no magic wands, and change isn't easy, but if you take it step by step and are consistent with your practice, you will reap the benefits of building resilience and incorporate it as a lifelong practice.

I believe that we can all build resilience within ourselves by adopting some very simple but powerful habits—a personal resilience code. While I firmly believe adopting these habits will build the resilience we need, I also understand that for most of us, this will be a lifelong journey. And as long as we continue to practice these habits, our story is not over—*we* get to write the ending. Resilience is an essential quality for navigating life's inevitable challenges, bouncing back from adversity, and thriving in the face of difficulties—which all of us face from time to time.

Now, let's dig a little deeper.

## The Science of Resilience

So, when life gets tough, how do you respond? Do you rise to the occasion, or do you let obstacles get in the way? How do you handle life's toughest moments? Do you find strength in adversity, or do you let challenges weigh you down?

Resilience is the skill that helps you bounce back from setbacks and thrive despite difficulties. But resilience isn't just about surviving tough times. It's about developing the mental and emotional strength to face them head-on and also be able to quickly respond to opportunities when they arise. You don't need resilience only to deal with the bad things that happen in your life, but also the good things that happen. Both take strength of character, mind, and body.

Clearly, resilience is a critical quality for overcoming life's challenges and emerging stronger than ever. It's the ability to adapt and thrive despite adversity and stress. It's a muscle that can be trained and strengthened over time. Resilience allows you to navigate difficulties, maintain a positive outlook, and keep pushing forward. You probably won't be surprised to learn that the brain plays a pivotal role in the amount of resilience we are able to bring to the table at any given time—combining psychology, neurobiology, human behavior, and many other fields.

## Resilience as a Personality Trait

*Resilience* is the ability of an individual, team, organization, family, or community to adapt successfully in the face of significant shocks, stressors, and threats to their normal function, viability, or development. From a scientific perspective, resilience consists of all the various processes that enable people to bounce back from difficult or challenging life experiences and continue moving forward.

The good news is that resilience is something that can be learned and developed over the course of a lifetime. According to psychologist Ann Masten, one of the preeminent researchers in the field of resilience, "As I studied children and families dealing with war, disasters, poverty, violence, and homelessness, I found a consistent set of surprisingly ordinary but powerful factors at work. Resilience didn't depend on special qualities but on a capacity to adapt that we develop over time as we are nurtured, learn, and gain experience."[1]

Resilience is not a static personality trait, something that always remains the same. Instead, it is a dynamic process that is ever-changing and emerges over time. Yes, some portion of the resilience we possess is a product of our genetics—the information encoded into our DNA. However, just as important are the environmental and experiential events that take place in our lives.

When we dig a bit deeper into the term *resilience*, we find that researchers describe different kinds of resilience, including psychological resilience, emotional resilience, and physical resilience. Each one of these dimensions relates to someone or something's ability to bounce back from a challenge, opportunity, or obstacle in their environment. Let's take a closer look at some different contexts for resilience in people and organizations.

## Individual Resilience

When scientists study resilience at the individual level, they are often looking at it in the context of childhood development. Early research in this area explored the characteristics that helped some children flourish despite being exposed to significant risks, such as poverty, abuse, or natural disasters. These protective factors include internal assets such as an easy temperament, positive emotions, and cognitive flexibility, and external assets such as supportive relationships and community resources. Each is important to the development and maintenance of strong individual resilience.

In a paper on the topic, researchers Ann Masten and Auke Tellegen say, "Resilience is not a superpower, but an everyday process that emerges from normal human adaptational systems."[2] In other words, instead of thinking of resilient people as special or out of the ordinary, it's better to think about resilience as a common capacity—a capacity that each and every one of us already possesses to some degree—that can be fostered and cultivated. It's what happens when basic human adaptational systems such as attachment, learning, and self-regulation operate at a level of efficiency that is higher than average.

## Family Resilience

Within families, resilience most often refers to the processes by which families endure and bounce back from adversity, and most families go through plenty of that. Family resilience encompasses such things as a positive view of the future, adaptive communication, collaborative problem-solving, and supportive behavior that enables families to adapt to challenges and support one another through crises—and to take on opportunities as they arise.

Simone Biles's biological mother, Shannon, was unable to care for Simone and her three siblings, and when Simone was six years old, they were placed in foster care. Three years later, her grandparents—Ronald and Nellie Biles—adopted Simone and her younger sister Adria, while her older siblings were adopted by their great-aunt. Ronald and Nellie loved and supported Simone every step of the way as she conquered the sport of women's gymnastics. They even built a gym—the World Champions Centre, in Spring, Texas—for her and other high-level gymnasts to train in.

Referring to her adoptive parents, Ronald and Nellie, Simone said, "My parents saved me. They've set huge examples of how to treat other people and they've been there to support me since day one. There's nothing I could say to them to thank them enough."[3]

Family resilience is affected by cultural, social, and economic factors. Families that have strong social support networks, material resources, and access to community are more likely to have the resilience they need to bounce back from the challenges and difficulties they encounter. Family resilience emphasizes the interdependence of family relationships and family members' ability to support and help one another.

## Community Resilience

Community resilience takes the idea of resilience and extends it to the collective capacity of communities to deal with and recover from challenges of all kinds, both good and bad. According to research, there are two primary ways of approaching community resilience: the social-ecological approach and the mental health and developmental psychology approach. The social-ecological approach focuses on social-ecological dependencies, while the mental health approach focuses on psychological and social support mechanisms that can foster healthy communities.

Whatever approach you take, when it comes to communities, resilience is the capacity to absorb, adapt to, prepare for, and recover from risks, shocks, and stresses. And community resilience comes in many forms—natural, physical, social, and economic. At the core of community resilience is the capacity of a community itself to anticipate, prepare for, respond to, and recover from adverse events and natural hazards, economic downturns, and social upheavals.

I'll never forget the time I visited my friend Cedric Richmond, then a member of the Louisiana legislature, just days after Hurricane Katrina devastated New Orleans. The entire neighborhood was pitch black, and we literally had to drive his car up to the front door of the house with headlights on in order to assess the damage. Cedric drove me downtown and past City Hall where windows had been blown out of office buildings. New Orleans is one of my favorite cities in the world, not simply for the cuisine, the music, and the culture, but because of the remarkable display of resilience the people and the city demonstrated in the wake of Katrina—and every day.

There's no doubt that many communities have been tested, some over and over again. Whether it's budget shortfalls; natural disasters such as hurricanes, tornados, drought, wildfires—or even the lingering aftereffects of the COVID-19 pandemic—our communities are being stressed like never before. It's up to us to do our part to make our communities more resilient and better able to survive and thrive today and long into the future.

## Organizational Resilience

Indeed, given that organizations are made up of individuals, it is perhaps no big surprise that resilience has now become a core part of the discussion. Organizational resilience is the capacity of an organizational system to adapt and recover from change and disruptions, and it's little wonder that organizations of all kinds—for-profits, nonprofits, and governmental—are now being encouraged to build resilience. This trait is widely considered to be crucial to flourishing in the long run, not only for organizational performance, but also employee well-being, happiness, and engagement. The most resilient organizations have a culture that fosters adaptability, innovation, and collaboration.

Strategies for building organizational resilience include cultivating a culture that nurtures the people who work there, facilitates flexibility, encourages ongoing learning and development, and makes it safe to fail. Organizations that are resilient are better able to absorb change and challenges, such as business cycles (for example, recessions and stock market fluctuations), technological disruption, and global crises (such as the COVID-19 pandemic).

In fact, during the COVID-19 pandemic, many businesses had to tap their deep wells of resilience just to keep the lights on. For example, the restrictions on travel that vacationers faced in early 2020 were a disaster for Airbnb—decimating its revenue model. In response, the company dramatically cut costs, raised funds, and put the emphasis on selling long-term stays and remote work. These actions enabled Airbnb to recover 70 percent of its business by summer 2020—paving the way for its successful IPO in December 2020.[4] And Walmart made the decision to charter its own fleet of ships—directing them to ports that weren't jammed with traffic—to keep merchandise moving into its more than ten thousand stores worldwide.[5]

When the world was changing all around them, these companies and many others chose to make lemonade out of that big pile of lemons.

That's resilience!

## Resilience Now and in the Future

From resilience in individuals and families to resilience in communities and organizations, the science of resilience can help us create more supportive environments. It does this by showing us what factors lead to resilience and by revealing strategies to enhance resilience—helping individuals and systems to better withstand the inevitable storms of our fast-changing world. As the research into resilience continues to develop, the challenge will be to integrate knowledge from different fields to develop a more comprehensive model and better understand the impact of resilience on human well-being and development.

As we look to the future of humanity, I can't help but wonder how artificial intelligence (AI) will enhance or detract from our ability to build resilience or if it will have any impact at all.

From what I can see, AI struggles to understand or replicate the complexity of human resilience—of course, it's still in its formative stages. Even today's most advanced technology can't begin to grasp or embody resilience the way humans can. Resilience is a powerful and deeply human quality that is a superpower for us because it relies on emotional strength, intuition, experience, and adaptability. At this time, AI works on patterns and logic and, therefore, struggles to replicate these very human traits. But I have no doubt that this will change in time.

Now more than ever, humans will need to develop their resilience because, whether we like it or not, whether we're prepared for it or not, AI is becoming an ever-larger part of our lives. As we grow together over the coming years and decades, resilience might just be *the* key differentiator between humans and machines. So, it's going to be in our best interest to continue to deepen our wells of resilience over the long term, maintaining and growing our uniquely human qualities in the process.

Regardless of where this technology goes, resilience is a key trait for facing the curveballs of life, bouncing back from adversity, and flourishing in the face of difficulty. Besides, when we are resilient, we are better equipped to keep our chin up, cope with the stress we feel, and refuse to quit in our efforts to reach for our goals. Those who are resilient are best able to keep their eyes on the prize—to learn from their failures and adapt to circumstances that are constantly changing.

And ultimately, that's how we win.

## Conclusion

Resilience is one of the most important qualities for thriving in life. While there are those who are more resilient by nature than others, resilience is a skill that can be learned and developed. Your ability to build resilience doesn't end until you do. Developing greater resilience involves building on traits such as social support, sense of purpose, flexibility, self-awareness, self-care, problem-solving, emotional resilience, realistic optimism, courage, and a growth mindset.

The code for resilience I present in this book consists of eight powerful habits you can and should learn, adopt, and do more of in your daily life. In the chapters that follow, I drill deep into each one of these habits and how you can put them to work in your own career, business, and life—leading you to the success you so richly deserve:

- Attitude
- Work ethic
- Agility
- Vulnerability
- Network
- Focus
- Dogged determination
- Faith

Resilience is like a muscle. The more we work it—deliberately, intentionally, consciously—the stronger it will become. Practicing resilience will make us more flexible, more gritty, more resilient. Life and business will never be without its struggles, but resilience will help us turn those experiences into opportunities to emerge as better versions of ourselves. We can't always control what happens to us, but we can control how we respond. That is the most important thing about resilience.

When we deliberately cultivate the habits and character traits that promote resilience, we are creating a set of inner resources we can draw on whenever we need them. This not only benefits us as individuals but also our families and communities, our businesses and customers, and the world at large. Resilient people lead to resilient organizations and societies, and that's something we'll always need more of.

I hope you'll remember the words of Dr. Martin Luther King Jr., who said, "Change does not roll in on the wheels of inevitability but comes through continuous struggle." It's resilience that enables us to make big changes happen. It's what gives us hope for the future and the power to do something about it.

Choose courage over comfort, and you'll never go wrong.

Now, let's get to work.

# CHAPTER 2

# Attitude

Attitude is a mindset, and the mind is so much more powerful than we can even imagine. But sometimes, especially when in the throes of uncertainty, upheaval, anxiety, worry, and change, it's hard to believe in the power of a positive mindset. Sometimes, the thought of keeping a positive attitude can feel exhausting or even insulting when you're facing overwhelming circumstances.

As I write this book, I'm seeing news of entire communities devastated by Hurricane Helene—people who have lost everything and are living day to day in shock with no idea what the future may bring. According to news reports, at least 223 people died because of the storm, hundreds of people were unaccounted for, and the physical damage is in the tens of billions of dollars.[1] I can't imagine that anyone in that situation wants to hear, "Just keep a positive attitude!" when what they really want and need are immediate aid and a sense of normalcy.

However, even in our darkest, most frightening, and uncertain moments, attitude is the truest form of resilience, and it can carry us so, so far. Because even in the toughest times or the worst of failures, your attitude wires your brain's response to what's in front of you and plays a key role in your survival mechanism.

This isn't wishful thinking; it's science. For example, a 2022 study by the National Institutes of Health on patient attitudes toward treatment for chronic illnesses found links between optimism and improved health outcomes.[2] Furthermore, a 2019 study by researchers at the Harvard School of Public Health links optimism with a longer life span.[3] So, while it may seem far-fetched and the last thing you want to hear in a time of crisis, you are in control of your thoughts, your attitude, and your optimism, and how you harness and utilize these thoughts has a measurable impact on outcomes.

A positive attitude is a key habit in your resilience code. How will a positive attitude increase your resilience and propel you to the success you so richly deserve?

Let's find out!

## The Power of Attitude

Rev. Jesse Jackson once said, "The ground is no place for a champion." If you and I were fighting and you knocked me out, that's kind of on you. But if you come back next week and I'm still on the ground, that's on me. This is the essence of attitude and grit. At some point, you've got to say to yourself, "You know, things may be bad right now, but somewhere inside there's a switch that I have the power to flip. If I flip this attitude switch, then everything else is going to start to change." I've experienced this for myself many times in my business, career, and personal life.

It's not only about overcoming adversity—our general attitude affects how we see the world around us. One person may look out the window on a gray day, woefully wishing it were sunnier. Another may appreciate how the cooler temperature allows them to better enjoy their walk. So much about the steps we take and how we achieve success is based on attitude and disposition. And having a positive attitude is a key ingredient in the recipe for building resilience.

Optimists and pessimists see the glass differently, either half full or half empty. Optimists have a more resilient perspective than pessimists, who tend to mostly focus on the negative. You simply cannot maintain a negative outlook and poor attitude and expect to be resilient in the face of life's challenges—resilience and pessimism are incompatible.

But cultivating a certain attitude, one that allows you to be resilient, is not exactly something you pick up in a store or something you can hold in your hands. It is something you have to embody and make part of your essence. And this is not easy for some people. Those who have been coddled, loved, and began life already on third base might have a hard time understanding others who have been crushed by life's circumstances.

Interestingly, those who had to scrap their way from first to third base, who had to duck and weave around countless obstacles along the way, can develop a resilience that far exceeds that of those for whom success came easily—who started out on third base. When the going gets tough, those who started ahead can often crumble, while those who know adversity and have built a deep well of resilience are able to shrug it off.

If you want to build a positive attitude—and your resilience—there are a variety of practical tools that can help, and being around other people who have been through challenges along the way to success is a good place to start. They don't panic when they're knocked down because they've been knocked down before and have gotten back up again. That experience of failure makes failing again less scary.

In the end, resilience is an act of will. Resilience is how we protect who we are—dreamers, believers, doers—in a world that might like to beat us out of that if it could. It is the power within us that allows us to take the bumps and bruises of life and still move on, bruises and all. Whether as leaders or individuals, it just might be the most critical characteristic for sustaining hope in an uncertain world.

## Demitrea Kelley and the Power of Resilience

Demitrea Kelley is a diversity and health advocate at Mid-Minnesota Legal Aid—supporting diverse communities in accessing healthcare and legal services—and she is the cofounder and CEO of the Mikayla Sarai Foundation. A LinkedIn profile written about her says that Demitrea's "story is fueled by advocacy, resilience, and passion."[4] And while her story is an inspiring and impressive one, it's Demitrea's founding of the Mikayla Sarai Foundation that really stands out.

You see, Mikayla Sarai is Demitrea's daughter, and the foundation was created to address the challenges of sickle cell disease (SCD)—with which Mikayla has struggled her entire life—while championing for a future where health equity is social justice. By the time she reached the age of fifteen, Mikayla had been hospitalized more than one hundred times.

To help everyone touched by this devastating disease, Demitrea dug deep into her resilience and took action. As she explains, "When my daughter was sick, I always felt we were getting the runaround. There were so many issues that required me to constantly advocate on her behalf with doctors, teachers, and social workers. From there, I decided I needed to figure out what I could do to advocate at the next level. I felt there needed to be policy changes, law changes, and all that happens at the legislative level. I decided to learn the law." So Demitrea is doing just that—on top of everything else, she is currently pursuing a JD degree at the Mitchell Hamline School of Law.

Demitrea demonstrates the power of a positive attitude—refusing to let anything prevent her from achieving her goals and aspirations. She has set the bar high, and she continues to inspire those around her. Demitrea lives and breathes the advice that she gives to her daughter. "I always tell Mikayla to keep going."

## Seven Ways to Adopt a Positive Attitude and Increase Your Resilience

Cultivating a positive attitude is a journey that involves conscious effort and practice. It's about training your mind to focus on the bright side, even in challenging circumstances. By incorporating techniques like mindfulness, gratitude, journaling, surrounding yourself with positive influences, and more, you can gradually shift your perspective and experience increased happiness and resilience. Remember, it's a process, and small steps can lead to significant changes over time.

So, how can you adopt a positive attitude? Here are some suggestions:

### 1. Practice Gratitude

Gratitude is one of the most powerful tools for shifting your mindset from negative to positive. By regularly expressing appreciation for the good things in your life, you train your brain to focus more on what's going right rather than wasting time and energy dwelling on problems or setbacks.

Practicing gratitude is a powerful way to shift your focus from what's wrong to what's right in your life. And while I personally gained much from my Twenty-Two Days of Gratitude, another effective way to cultivate gratitude is by keeping a gratitude journal. This involves writing down some things you're thankful for each day, no matter how small they may seem. Reflecting on the good things in your life can help you appreciate what you have and gain a more positive outlook.

Over time, this daily practice rewires your brain to more naturally notice and savor life's positives. You start to see each day through a lens of abundance rather than scarcity. Challenges feel more manageable because your attention is on your resources rather than your limitations.

Research has shown that practicing gratitude can have a significant impact on both physical and mental health. Studies have found that people who practice gratitude on a regular basis tend to have lower blood pressure, stronger immune systems, and fewer chronic illnesses. They also tend to have higher levels of happiness, life satisfaction, and social connections.

To start a gratitude journal, choose a notebook or digital tool that works for you and commit to writing in it at the same time every day. It could be first thing in the morning, before bed, or during your lunch break. Write down three things you're grateful for and try to be as specific as possible. For example, instead of just writing "My coworkers," or "My friends," you could write "My team partner who always knows how to make me laugh," or "My friends who bring so much joy and energy to my life."

It's also important to mix it up and not merely focus on the same things every day. Try to think about different areas of your life, such as your relationships, health, career, and personal growth. You can also include things that may seem small or insignificant, such as a good cup of coffee, a beautiful sunset, or a warm shower.

In addition to writing in a gratitude journal, you can also express gratitude in other ways, such as sharing your gratitude with a friend or loved one, writing a thank-you note, or simply taking a moment to reflect on the good things in your life.

Here are some specific tips:

- **Specificity is key.** Instead of writing generic entries like "I'm grateful for my family," be specific. For example, "I'm grateful for the heartfelt laughter we shared during dinner tonight." This level of detail enhances the positive impact of gratitude journaling.

- **Variety is essential.** To prevent your gratitude journal from becoming monotonous and boring, explore different aspects of your life. Express gratitude for your health, relationships, achievements, experiences, and even small joys like a hummingbird flying outside your window or a delicious meal.

- **Overcoming challenges.** Some days, finding things to be grateful for might seem difficult. In these moments, focus on the small things, such as having a roof over your head, food on your table, or the ability to breathe. Remember, gratitude is a muscle that strengthens with practice.

## 2. Reframe Negative Thoughts

Negative experiences are inevitable, but how we interpret and respond to them determines their ultimate impact on our attitude. Cognitive reframing is a technique for shifting perspective on adverse events to extract insight and meaning from them.

For example, getting passed over for a promotion could be seen as a sign that you'll never advance in your career. However, you could instead reframe it as valuable feedback on skills to develop, so you'll be better positioned for new opportunities. Failing to reach a goal could mean that you're a hopeless failure—or it could mean that you're stretching beyond your comfort zone and learning important lessons in the process. You can also try to focus on the present moment and what you can control rather than getting caught up in worries about the future or regrets about the past. Mindfulness practices, such as meditation and deep breathing, can help you stay present and focused.

With practice, you can train yourself to reframe knee-jerk negative reactions into more constructive interpretations. Ask yourself what you can learn from difficult experiences. Look for the hidden opportunity or silver lining in disappointing situations. Over time, seeing the good in the bad becomes more automatic. This isn't about sugarcoating reality or denying your feelings—it's about zooming out to see the bigger picture. You can't always control what happens to you, but you can control how you respond.

Cognitive reframing involves changing the way you interpret negative situations. Instead of seeing setbacks as failures, view them as opportunities to learn and grow. This can help you develop a more positive attitude and build resilience.

Here are some specific tips:

- **Identify negative thoughts.** Pay attention to your thought patterns. When you notice negative self-talk, question its validity. Is there evidence to support this thought? Is there an alternative perspective?

- **Challenge negative beliefs.** Once you've identified a negative thought, challenge its accuracy. Are you making generalizations based on limited information? Are you catastrophizing? Are you engaging in all-or-nothing thinking?

- **Develop positive alternatives.** Replace negative thoughts with more balanced and optimistic ones. For example, instead of thinking, *I'm such a failure*, try *This didn't go as planned, but I can learn from this experience.*

## 3. Surround Yourself with Positivity

The people we spend time with and the environments we put ourselves in have a huge influence over our own attitudes and emotions. You've probably noticed how your mood and energy are affected by the emotional tone of those around you. Attitudes are contagious.

That's why it's so important to be intentional about the company you keep and the places you go. Surround yourself with positive, inspiring people who bring out the best in you. Limit time with chronic complainers or pessimists who drag down your mood and motivation. Connect with mentors and role models whose lives embody the attitude you want to emulate.

This may mean setting boundaries with the toxic people in your work and life who drain your energy or make you feel bad about yourself. It may also mean seeking out new relationships or activities that bring you joy and fulfillment.

In addition to the people you surround yourself with, your physical environment can also have a big impact on your attitude. Create a physical environment that both uplifts and energizes you. Declutter and organize your space in a way that makes it feel good to be in. Display photos, art, quotes, and objects that are meaningful and inspiring to you. Optimize lighting, temperature, scent, and sound to create an ambiance that promotes positivity.

By consciously curating the influences you allow into your life, you create an ecosystem that supports a positive attitude. You make it easier to stay inspired, motivated, and optimistic.

Proactively design a life that keeps you in a positive frame of mind.

Here are some specific tips:

- **Choose your circle wisely.** Evaluate the people in your life. Do they contribute positively to your well-being? Do they support your goals and dreams?

- **Build strong connections.** Nurture your relationships with positive and supportive people. Spend quality time together, engage in shared activities, and offer genuine support.

- **Let go of toxic relationships.** It's essential to recognize when a relationship is no longer serving you. Don't be afraid to set boundaries or distance yourself from toxic individuals.

## 4. Set Realistic Goals

Having meaningful goals to work toward fuels optimism and motivation. It gives you a compelling reason to push through obstacles. The key is to set realistic goals that strike a balance between being challenging and achievable.

Unrealistic goals set you up for frustration and self-doubt. On the flip side, goals that are too easy lead to stagnation and boredom. The sweet spot is where you have to stretch yourself and develop new skills, but you can see a clear path forward with hard work.

Breaking down larger goals into smaller, manageable steps can help you build confidence and reinforce a positive attitude. Achieving these smaller milestones can give you a sense of accomplishment and motivation to keep moving forward.

To set realistic goals, start by identifying what you want to achieve and why. Make sure your goals are specific, measurable, and aligned with your values. Then break down your larger goals into smaller, actionable steps.

For example, let's say you want to start a new business. Instead of feeling overwhelmed by the enormity of the task, break it down into smaller steps—such as researching your market, creating a business plan, securing funding, and setting up a website or Instagram for your business. Celebrate your progress along the way to keep yourself energized and encouraged. Dwelling only on the end goal can be overwhelming. Take time to appreciate how far you've come and what you're learning in the process.

If you fall short of a goal, adopt a growth mindset, seeing it as an opportunity to learn and improve rather than an indictment of your abilities. Embrace challenges as chances to get stronger and wiser. Cultivate grit and persistence to keep showing up even when it's hard.

Having a clear sense of purpose, along with a step-by-step road map to get there, naturally generates hope and positivity. It gives you agency to create the life you want. Commit to the process and have faith in your ability to figure things out.

Here are some specific tips:

- **Define your goals.** Clearly articulate your goals. What do you want to achieve? Why is it important to you?

- **Set SMART goals.** Ensure your goals are specific, measurable, achievable, relevant, and time-bound.

- **Create a plan.** Develop a step-by-step plan to reach your goals. Break down larger goals into smaller, manageable tasks.

- **Celebrate milestones.** Acknowledge and celebrate your achievements, no matter how small. This reinforces positive behavior and boosts your motivation.

## 5. Engage in Positive Self-Talk

How you speak to yourself is important. Negative self-talk is an energy-sucking, self-esteem–depleting habit. Expressions such as "I can't do this" and "I'm such an idiot" are self-fulfilling prophecies. If you don't believe in yourself, how will you take positive risks or persist in the face of adversity?

To turn this around, first become more mindful of what you're telling yourself. Is your self-talk positive or negative? If it's negative, then reframe your inner monologue by taking note of your self-critical statements and deliberately replacing them with positive, empowering affirmations.

Instead of "This will never work," say "I can make this work, one step at a time."

Instead of "I'm not good enough," say "I'm capable and constantly improving."

Instead of "I always screw up," say "I'm doing the best I can and learning invaluable lessons."

Talk to yourself as you would a good friend—with kindness, with respect, and by believing in your abilities. Recall occasions when you've overcome challenges in the past. Believe in your strength and tenacity.

Here are some specific tips:

- **Identify negative self-talk.** Notice what your inner critic says. What are you telling yourself?

- **Create positive affirmations.** Come up with positive affirmations to counteract negative self-talk. Affirmations should be specific, positive, and believable.

- **Practice regularly.** Repeat your affirmations daily, visualizing yourself as the person you aspire to be.

- **Believe in yourself.** To work, affirmations need to be believable—and achievable.

## 6. Practice Mindfulness and Meditation

Mindfulness is nonjudgmental awareness of what's happening in the here and now, and it is the cure for the pain and stress of ruminating over the past and worrying about the future—the two most powerful forms of negativity.

Meditation is a mindfulness technique. Generally, you focus your attention on your breathing or a mantra, and when you find that your mind has wandered off, you bring it back. Through repetition, you get better at observing your thoughts and feelings without getting lost in them.

This is what enables you to respond more skillfully to challenges rather than react impulsively—you can see what's in front of you more clearly, without the added layers of narrative drama and anxiety that arise from both your own fears and projections. Meditation also enables you to savor positive experiences more fully in the moment.

In fact, research shows that the more you meditate regularly, the more your brain changes, strengthening those regions involved with positive emotions and weakening those involved with stress and negativity. A few minutes a day can make a big difference in how you feel and think.

You can bring mindfulness into everyday activities such as eating, walking, and even conversation. Bring your full attention to what you are doing, using all your five senses. Notice when your attention strays into the past or the future and gently return it to the present.

Mindfulness helps you to step off the frantic, never-ending treadmill of mental chatter and reconnect with the pure aliveness of being here and now. It's a way to halt the negative momentum and savor the magic of ordinary life.

Here are some specific tips:

- **Practice mindful breathing.** Set aside a few minutes

every day to pay attention to your breath. This technique can quiet the mind and reduce stress.

- **Try a body scan meditation.** Bring your attention to different parts of your body, noticing whatever sensations are there and labeling them without judgment, such as "Here is the sensation of feeling the skin on the back of my neck."

- **Engage in mindful walking.** Attend to the sensations of walking, the sounds around you, and what you see.

## 7. Engage in Physical Activity

Take care of your body. You can't expect to be upbeat and resilient if your body isn't in good shape. Your physical health has a direct correlation to your mental and emotional health. It's a lot harder to keep up a positive attitude when you're sleep-deprived or always planted on the sofa watching TV.

One of the best ways to improve your mood and energy is to exercise regularly. When you exercise, your brain releases endorphins, powerful neurochemicals that decrease stress and promote a happy, euphoric feeling.

Exercise also helps you to blow off steam, clear your head, and break unproductive thought loops. Moving your body reduces muscle tension, helps with sleep quality, and gives you a sense of mastery and self-efficacy.

You don't need to run a marathon to get them either—just moderate activity such as walking or dancing will do. Find something you enjoy and do it regularly. Make it something you don't have a choice about—like brushing your teeth.

Pay attention to your overall physical health. Consume healthy meals that keep your blood sugar and energy levels in balance, stay hydrated to help your brain function at its best, and aim for seven to nine hours of sleep per night. Take breaks to stretch and move.

When you feel strong, energized, and well-rested, you show up to your life with more positivity. Self-care is ultimately a form of self-love; when you're taking care of your body, you are telling your subconscious that you're important and deserve respect.

Here are some specific tips:

- **Find an activity you enjoy.** Pick an exercise you like, such as dancing, swimming, hiking, tennis—*anything*.

- **Set realistic goals.** Aim for shorter, easier workouts at first, then increase their intensity and duration over time.

- **Make it a habit.** Find ways to incorporate exercise into your daily life. Schedule your workouts and enlist the help of an exercise buddy to keep you accountable.

## Conclusion

Cultivating a positive attitude is an ongoing practice, not a one-and-done event—it's a journey, not a destination. When you take the steps described in this chapter and begin to feel less victimized, more empowered, and happier, you will face the future with greater optimism as your resilience grows.

Remember, you don't need to do everything at once. Pick one or two habits and get started, adding to your arsenal of positivity over time. Go gently with yourself and savor your achievements along the way. Some days will be harder than others. Progress is not always a straight line. You will have setbacks and rough patches. But what matter most are your commitment to keep moving forward and your willingness to keep showing up and doing your best.

Of all the gifts you can give yourself, a positive attitude is one of the most valuable. It's what shapes the quality and tone of your life experience. Be patient with yourself, and kind. Reward the effort, not just the achievement. Find people and resources that will help you grow. Over time, having an optimistic, positive attitude will come naturally to you. You will feel more resilient, more purposeful, and more alive.

# CHAPTER 3

# Work Ethic

I don't think there are any organizations more deeply embedded in the civil rights movement than the Southern Christian Leadership Conference (SCLC). The organization was founded in 1957 by Dr. Martin Luther King Jr. and other activists in response to the ongoing injustice of racial segregation in the United States. The SCLC was instrumental in organizing nonviolent protests, voter registration, and advocating for the rights of Black people, especially in the South. Under Dr. King's leadership, the SCLC played major roles in the Birmingham protests, the 1963 March on Washington—where King gave his famous "I Have a Dream" speech—marches in Selma and Montgomery, and much more.

The organization's concerted and unrelenting efforts put pressure on Congress and President Lyndon Johnson, leading to passage of the Civil Rights Act of 1964 and the Voting Rights Act of 1965. And the SCLC continued its work, even after Dr. King was assassinated in Memphis in 1968—advocating for social justice and equality while fighting economic inequality and poverty.

So you can imagine that I was enormously honored and excited when I was handpicked by Martin Luther King III—the son of Dr. Martin Luther King Jr. and president of the SCLC—in 2001 to join this fabled organization as national executive director and chief operating officer.

I was just twenty-seven years old—a young whippersnapper working with many of the civil rights heroes who had carried the SCLC forward after the untimely death of its founder but had never fully recovered from the tragic event. My charge was to come in and advance this organization and this movement to a new generation, the men and women who would one day take the place of the SCLC's old guard, and I worked hard from day one to do just that.

It was a heady experience. There I was, sitting in Dr. King's office on Auburn Avenue in Atlanta, on much the same path that many of my own civil rights heroes had walked before me. I graduated from Morehouse College—the world's only all-male, historically Black college that Martin Luther King Jr., Maynard Jackson, Julian Bond, Spike Lee, Samuel Jackson, A. Benjamin Spencer, Dr. Delman L. Coates, and many other distinguished individuals had attended—and I had earned my master of divinity from Princeton Theological Seminary.

But it all came crashing down when, just six months later, Martin Luther King III was suspended by the SCLC's board of directors, and I was fired in the resulting, very public dustup. While King was eventually reinstated by the board, I was not. So there I was—a stunned, out-of-work young man who was unsure what to do next.

As Kent Matlock, the founder of a marketing and PR agency that did work for the SCLC at the time—and who served on the SCLC board—explains in an interview, "Lamell left under terrible circumstances that had nothing to do with his performance. There was resistance with the old guard to a young man bringing in fresh ideas and a new level of professionalism. The experience was unfair, but Lamell didn't dwell on that. He found a way out of it."

After returning home from a trip to South Africa to promote the latest installment of the blockbuster film *Rush Hour 2* with my friend, comedian Chris Tucker, I decided to Google myself (Google was still a fairly new tool to get news and information) and see what turned up. The result was story after story about the twenty-seven-year-old man—*me*—who had been handpicked by Martin Luther King III to help him run the SCLC and was fired from that organization six months later. At that moment, I determined that there was no way God intended that to be the final word for my life and legacy.

So, while the path I was on had turned into a dead end, I needed to figure out an entirely new one. Through my time in the office of Congressman Jesse Jackson Jr. as a congressional intern on Capitol Hill while at Princeton Seminary; my job right out of graduate school working with James Compton at the Chicago Urban League; my time at Rainbow/PUSH as a travel assistant to his dad, Rev. Jesse Jackson Sr.; and my position with Martin Luther King III at SCLC; I had built relationships with entrepreneurs and business owners across the country and around the world, and I decided to start a business of my own.

I looked into different franchises and even considered the idea of founding a car dealership, but ultimately, I realized that those endeavors weren't where my passion was. I needed to find something that would allow me to marry my passion for advocacy with the spirit of entrepreneurship.

Growing up on the South Side of Chicago, I had developed deep political instincts and relationships over the years. Some of the people with whom I had built relationships weren't necessarily professional lobbyists, but they were people who spent their lives advocating on behalf of folks with local, state, and federal government organizations.

Frankly, as I think about it, I can't help but draw a direct connection to my current career in policy and politics to the hours spent as a young high school student at Whitney Young High School in meetings with adults participating in the policymaking process. There were local school council meetings that I attended after school; voter registration and education drives at Operation PUSH with my mentor and the man who sent me to Morehouse College, Rev. Tyrone Crider; and mayoral campaigns for Danny Davis. Rev. Willie Taplin Barrow always made sure I had scholarship money, and I was a forever admirer and student of Mayor Harold Washington.

So, when I decided to start a lobbying firm and moved from Atlanta to Washington, D.C., to build my practice from the ground up, it might have been unusual for the D.C. crowd of professional lobbyists, but I was just doing and being what I had always been taught to do.

One of my good friends in D.C. is Ray Anderson, a native of Chicago and also a child of Rainbow/PUSH. He was the director of Federal Legislative Relations for the Chicago Public Schools when I came up with the idea to start my firm in D.C. I asked him if I could stay at his place while I got my firm up and running.

"Hey," I told him, "I just need a place to sleep, and I won't bother you. Promise." He agreed, and for a year after I left the SCLC, I slept on his couch and scoured the city for opportunities—ultimately coming up with the idea of Perennial Strategy Group.

Make no mistake about it—building a lobbying firm in a city filled with lobbying firms is no easy feat. At the time, there were more than forty thousand registered lobbyists in Washington, D.C., and they had the credibility, expertise, background on Capitol Hill, and personal relationships in cabinet agencies and the White House that I lacked. But I was convinced that with hard work and determination, I could do it.

I hadn't made a name for myself in the city, so I realized that naming the firm McMorris and Associates or McMorris Consultants wouldn't mean anything to anyone there. But the thing I concluded about Washington was that everything in the city was all about monuments and longevity and history, so I wanted to send a message to the world that I was going to be a part of that ethos. I named the firm Perennial Strategy Group to signify that we would be around for years and would be aligned with the unique culture and fabric of Washington.

The next step was to find office space. Every big city has a major business thoroughfare. For Chicago, it's Michigan Avenue. For New York City, it's Fifth Avenue. For Atlanta, it's Peachtree Street. And if you want to be a lobbyist in Washington, D.C., then Pennsylvania Avenue is where it's at. And so, I started looking for office space around Pennsylvania Avenue between the White House and Capitol Hill.

In partnership with a realtor, I found a space at the Willard Offices, a commercial property located at 1455 Pennsylvania Avenue—adjacent to the Willard InterContinental Hotel and just a couple of steps from the White House. The lobbyist who had the space was retiring, and I moved in—with no staff, no furniture, and no clients. But with a lot of hard work, I was convinced I could and would change that.

As a side note, I learned soon after I moved into my office (another Google moment) that President Ulysses S. Grant used to sit in the lobby of the Willard Hotel, smoking a cigar and sipping a brandy. Grant was often hounded by people asking for jobs or legislative favors, and it's said he referred to them as "those damn lobbyists"—with a nod to the Willard lobby in which he sat.[1] I believe that if we're paying attention, God gives us confirmations that we're in the right place at the right time doing exactly what we've been called to do. The fact that I had landed at the Willard was just one of many confirmations in the face of adversity that my idea for a business was the right one at the right time and place.

The people who hired me early on were people I met along the way who didn't know me, didn't know my background, but decided to take a chance on me anyway. One exception to that rule was Doris Crenshaw, a civil rights activist and hero from Montgomery, Alabama, who I met while I was working as a college intern in Martin Luther King III's office when he was a Fulton County Commissioner in Atlanta. I was acquainted and connected with Martin and Doris even before my time at the SCLC.

Early on, Doris called me to a dinner at The Prime Rib steakhouse on K Street—K Street is another major hub for lobbying in D.C. Doris didn't tell me what her plan was for dinner, but when I arrived, there was a longtime lobbyist for Alabama Power seated at her table.

As the dinner progressed, Doris told this individual, "You need to give Lamell a contract."

Stunned, I sputtered, "What?"

Without missing a beat, the lobbyist simply replied, "OK." And that ended up being the beginning of the longest-standing client relationship with my new firm. Twenty-two years later, I'm still very close to all those folks. The lobbyist was Julian Smith; years later, I ended up working with his son Houston Smith, who's proudly continuing his dad's legacy at the power company.

Another pivotal event for my young firm was meeting John Milne. I used to eat dinner at the Oceanaire Seafood Room on F Street most every night—it was located right between my office and my apartment. I got to know another regular there,

John—I called him the mayor of Oceanaire—and we were from polar-opposite sides of the political spectrum. Ironically, we were both from Illinois, but he's from downstate in Farina, Illinois, and I'm from Chicago. He was a longstanding, well-known, and well-regarded D.C. lobbyist, and one evening, I asked him if he would consider joining me in trying to build out my firm.

"Yes," he quickly replied.

I was shocked, but as I reflect back to that moment in time, I think John must have said to himself, "Well, if this kid is crazy enough to start up a lobbying firm from scratch and put his office across the street from the White House, then I'm crazy enough to join him." He was best friends with the Speaker of the U.S. House of Representatives at the time, John Boehner, and he brought along a book of business that was the catalyst to growing my firm. When John came on board, that gave me the bona fides around town that I needed to launch Perennial Strategy Group—and later, Perennial Sports and Entertainment.

Ray Anderson recently commented on my extreme work ethic at the time, reminding me that I would leave his house at 6:00 a.m.—hustling for work, running down every lead I could, and taking every meeting with anyone I thought would help me get my career back on track. As he said, "I knew he lived there, but I never saw him. When I got up in the morning to get ready for work, Lamell was already gone, and he wouldn't get back until 9:00 or 10:00 p.m. It was just him being ambitious, hustling and looking to create the next opportunity to move his career forward."

With a lot of hard work, I was able to build a phenomenally successful business. Truth be told, there's no getting around hard work if you want to achieve anything good in your life, and that's why it's a key habit in your resilience code.

## The Power of Work Ethic

They say success is the sum of small efforts repeated day in and day out. It's a platitude, perhaps, but within the simplicity of this idea lies a profound truth. At the heart of this equation is a quality often overlooked with so much attention paid to talent and intelligence: work ethic. It's the unseen force that propels individuals beyond their limitations—both real and perceived— it's the crucible in which character is forged, and it's the constant companion on anyone's journey to long-term success.

A strong work ethic is more than just being busy—it's a mindset for getting things done, a philosophy of life. It's the quiet determination that drove me to rise before dawn when I landed in D.C. and persist long after others had given up. It's what transforms aspirations into tangible realities, turning dreams into results. With a strong work ethic as your foundation, you are empowered to set audacious goals, undeterred by the difficulty it may take to achieve them. You understand that the journey is not a sprint but a marathon, and it's the steady, consistent pace that ultimately wins the race.

Such dedication inevitably leaves an imprint on the people around you. A reputation for being someone with a strong work ethic is a powerful asset that can build trust and deliver opportunities to your front door. As word spreads about your reliability, commitment, and pursuit of excellence, doors will open for you, revealing alternatives previously obscured. Not only that, but each challenge conquered, each task mastered, is a catalyst for personal growth and your relentless pursuit of mastery.

Beyond the tangible rewards you'll earn along the way, a strong work ethic cultivates an intangible yet invaluable asset: a positive spirit. The satisfaction that stems from overcoming obstacles, from witnessing the fruits of your own labor, is tremendously powerful. It's the internal compass that guides you through the most difficult challenges and shows you the way forward. The optimism you gain from each success, like ripples in a pond, extends outward, inspiring those around you to work hard to reach their own potential.

But perhaps the most profound impact of a strong work ethic lies in its role as a builder of resilience. As we all know, our ride through life is rarely smooth and uneventful. It's more like a roller coaster with its share of exhilarating ups and depressing downs. It's in moments of adversity that the true character of an individual is revealed. A strong work ethic is the bedrock upon which resilience is constructed. It's the unwavering belief that challenges are not dead ends but detours—opportunities to learn, adapt, and grow.

When faced with setbacks, people who have a strong work ethic are less likely to be consumed by self-doubt. Instead, they view obstacles as puzzles to be solved, hurdles to be leaped over, and challenges to be overcome. They understand that perseverance is not merely a virtue but a necessity. With each challenge overcome, their confidence strengthens, and their resolve deepens.

The good news is that a strong work ethic is a muscle that can be strengthened through deliberate practice. It begins with clear, well-defined goals—the North Star that guides your journey. Breaking down these big goals into smaller, more easily achievable steps creates a roadmap to your success. But it's not enough to create this roadmap—to succeed, you must couple it with discipline, which is the ability to focus, eliminate distractions, and immerse yourself in the task at hand. And as we all know, there are all sorts of distractions in today's world to throw us off track.

Research shows that we lose an average of a little over two hours every workday due to distractions from phone calls, social media, talkative coworkers, alerts and popups on our computers, and all sorts of other reasons. In fact, we are usually able to focus on a task for only eleven minutes before we are distracted, and once distracted, it takes us around twenty-five minutes to return to the task.[2]

A support network is another vital component for your ability to embrace a strong work ethic. Surrounding yourself with people who share similar values and habits, who offer encouragement and accountability, can make the journey significantly less difficult. When your coworkers and friends constantly invite you to party with them—tearing you away from your work—it's going to be hard for you to find the success you so richly deserve. There's a time and a place for play, and we all need to cultivate a healthy work-life balance, but make sure it doesn't become your default option.

Having a strong work ethic builds resilience by helping you persevere through challenges and setbacks. When you're dedicated to your work, you don't give up easily when faced with obstacles. You have the mental toughness to keep pushing forward even when things get difficult. It's this grit and determination that allow people with a strong work ethic to ultimately succeed when others might quit.

To illustrate the power of work ethic, consider a few examples:

- A student who puts in long hours studying, completes extra practice problems, and asks questions when confused will likely outperform classmates who study less—even if those classmates are naturally gifted. The student's work ethic and discipline make all the difference.

- An entry-level employee impresses managers by always arriving early, assisting colleagues, and finding ways to go above and beyond her basic duties. Her work ethic gets her promoted over her coworkers with more experience but less drive.

- An entrepreneur faces hundreds of rejections and setbacks while trying to get his startup off the ground. However, his strong work ethic allows him to persevere and keep trying new approaches when most others would have given up. Eventually, he succeeds.

In each case, the individual's work ethic—the sum total of their determination, drive, and dedication—allows them to accomplish ambitious goals and outperform others. They demonstrate grit and resilience in the face of challenges, and they find the success they desire.

Ultimately, your work ethic is one of the most important factors in determining your long-term success. Unlike innate talent or sheer luck, it's something you can control and improve through your own efforts. By committing to self-discipline, professionalism, and always giving your best effort, you'll achieve more than you ever thought possible. A strong work ethic is a superpower that will serve you well throughout your life.

## Seven Ways to Embrace a Work Ethic That Will Increase Your Resilience

Embracing a strong work ethic is an important ingredient for building your resilience. But how exactly can you do that? Here are seven ways I personally have found to work very well for anyone who adopts them.

### 1. Put Yourself in Situations Where You Need to Adapt

I travel a lot for work. In any given week, I can be in five different cities, in several different time zones. And with travel, anything can go wrong—even the best-laid plans can be totally upended by a single twenty-minute delay. My ability to deal with near-constant travel and its ongoing challenges has helped me build up resilience that I can and do apply to all sorts of other challenges as well.

By purposefully putting yourself in situations where you might need to adapt and coming prepared with the tools to do so (apps updated, phone charged), you are learning from your mistakes while building out a more resilient character. Part of building resilience is learning to accept disruptions and find ways to be adaptable to them by thinking on your feet and improvising novel solutions.

This doesn't extend just to travel—you can put yourself in situations where you need to adapt in most every other part of your life. For example, you can develop a new hobby, make new friends, or take on a new role at work, all of which will expose you to new ways of doing things and thinking about the world. The more varied your experiences, the more resilient you become.

While hard work will help you find the success you desire, know that you will fail along the way. Learn from your failures and setbacks. When you face a challenge and fail, take the time to consider how things might have gone better, what you learned, and how you can apply that knowledge to future situations. When obstacles arise, which they will, see them as opportunities to grow.

Here are some specific tips:

- **Get out of your own way.** Purposefully put yourself in challenging, foreign spaces or situations that demand some on-the-fly thinking and adapting—for example, by trying new hobbies or activities, traveling to different countries (or even just a different part of town than you habitually frequent), or assuming new job responsibilities.

- **Practice spontaneity.** Decide on your plans, but try to be spontaneous along the way, perhaps changing your plans or stopping to "smell the roses" and enjoy a spur-of-the moment walk through the park or a game of golf or tennis with a business associate or friend.

- **Learn from your defeats.** Every problem is an opportunity to improve. Make a note of what went wrong, then apply the lessons you learn the next time you face the same problem.

## 2. Do Small Tasks That You Don't Like

I have a friend who hated to open her mail. While much of the mail we get nowadays seems to be junk (I think that's what keeps the postal service afloat), if there's anything in an envelope that's time-sensitive, it's better handled sooner than later. Which means you should be opening up that mail. But you wouldn't believe how hard this was for my friend. However, she committed to taking the small step of opening her mail every day, and in doing so, she was able to get things done while building resilience.

Building resilience isn't just about working hard on the big things; it also means working hard on the small stuff and getting things done. Try overcoming unhelpful avoidance patterns and procrastination that take time and energy from the work at hand. Pick the things you always put off and break them down into smaller steps. Overcoming the small things that you don't like—and making a habit of it—gradually makes it easier for you to overcome the big things you don't like.

Here are some specific tips:

- **Take note of your avoidance behaviors.** Write down the things you should be doing that you always manage to put off and then break them down into smaller, more manageable chunks. Overcoming your avoidance behaviors and succeeding in the completion of these mini challenges will fill the reservoir of resilience you need to take on and complete the bigger ones.

- **Cultivate mindfulness.** Attend to your thoughts and feelings as you deal with difficult tasks, assignments, and duties. This will help you observe your resistance more clearly and then find ways to overcome it.

- **Celebrate small wins.** Reward yourself for the successful completion of your small tasks—not just your big ones. Positive reinforcement can help you feel good about what's ahead.

## 3. Use Your Nondominant Hand

Doing things that push your brain to new limits can increase cognitive flexibility—the ability to adapt to new situations—and find creative solutions to tough problems at work and at home. When buffeted by strong winds, trees that sway are less likely to break. Researchers have found that people who are encouraged to cross-train their brains—doing such things as learning a second language, playing a musical instrument, or completing a jigsaw puzzle—tend to adjust more quickly to changing circumstances.

Cognitive flexibility can be enhanced through a conscious effort to seek out diverse views and perspectives. For instance, you might think carefully about an issue from the opposing side or try to look at a challenging situation through someone else's eyes. When you engage in this process of perspective-taking, you develop greater empathy and open-mindedness, and you can tackle problems more creatively because you're able to see them from multiple angles. This can ultimately help you work smarter and not just harder.

Here are some specific tips:

- **Cross-train your brain.** Learn a language, play a musical instrument, or do puzzles; cognitive flexibility, a crucial indicator of general cognition, can be enhanced through engagement with novel activities.

- **Look at things from a new perspective.** Actively seek out other perspectives. This builds empathy, open-mindedness, and the ability to see things from different angles.

- **See failure as an option.** Failure is a part of the learning process. Rather than seeing failure as something to steer away from, view failure as a positive element of learning.

## 4. Make a Point to Find the Answer Before You Ask the Question

Finding the answer before asking the question can save time and help you have more productive conversations—enabling you to focus your hard work on where it is needed the most. It also fosters independence. When you invest in finding out what you can find yourself, you cultivate a sense of your own critical thinking and problem-solving abilities, and you will start to get a sense for which sources are good and which are less so. All these things are worthwhile and useful in all kinds of settings, from home to work.

Even if you don't find the answer to your question in advance, the search itself might provide you with a wider array of knowledge about the topic. Sifting through the research can reveal context, nuances, and related concepts—leading to a deeper understanding of the issue. This can position you to ask more specific questions the next time you don't understand something, again allowing you to put the focus of your hard work where it will do the most good.

Here are some specific tips:

- **Question assumptions.** Look beneath the surface for the underlying truths behind the status quo and explore potential solutions to the problems you encounter. This fosters creativity and helps you come up with new approaches.
- **Build a knowledge bank.** Work on broadening your knowledge and skills through reading, workshops, or online courses so you can handle issues with confidence.
- **Seek mentorship.** Learn from experienced individuals who can provide guidance, support, and new perspectives.

## 5. Add One More Rep or One More Minute to Your Workout

Try to squeeze in one more rep or one more minute of exercise when you're at a loss for energy—it's guaranteed to help you grow. The place where a workout can make or break for you is inevitably at the end, when the voice in your head is most likely to say, "Now you've done enough," while a slightly stronger voice says, "There isn't much point stopping now—I still feel great." If you can force yourself to add one more rep or stay at the gym for just one more minute, it will be worth it, but that door is a hard one to push through.

That last little push is the key to the workout. No matter what you are seeking to achieve—better muscle tone, greater endurance, a higher level of fitness overall—those last few seconds of pushing, when you are past the threshold of comfort and into the zone of discomfort, are where you make the difference and challenge your body to grow, get strong, or get fit.

What's more, this extra push teaches you to control your thoughts, be resilient, and rise to a challenge. Mastering an extra rep or minute gives you a sense of power and resolve, which you can then take into the next workout's battle against the clock. So, next time you feel like quitting, reflect on the possible gain and give it a go, just a bit longer.

Here are some specific tips:

- **Set stretch goals.** Achievement occurs when goals are truly challenging. Stretch goals take us out of our comfort zone. Stretch goals build resilience.

- **Develop a growth mindset.** Believe that you can learn and improve, that your intelligence is a characteristic that you grow into. This will give you a positive attitude and help you persevere.

- **Cultivate self-care.** Look after your body and mind, exercising, eating well, and finding ways to relax. A strong base means you can bounce back.

## 6. Set Aside Time Every Day to Take In What You're Seeing and Hearing

Find time each day to take in what is around you and what you hear, even if you feel there is nothing there. We live in a world filled with intense inputs—notifications screaming for attention, endless demands at our jobs, and a maddening insistence on constant connectivity. All this and more can leave us feeling overloaded, rushed, and disconnected from the very world around us. Taking the time—say, every day for even five minutes—to just sit and observe and listen is crucial for the soul and building the mental energy we need to do work over a sustained period of time.

The rewards of taking the time to see and hear the world around us are many. First, it reduces levels of stress. Bringing our attention into the present moment distracts us from thinking about the past or the future and allows our minds to rest for a while. Second, mindfulness increases our creativity. By paying attention to details, noticing patterns, and listening to what isn't always easy to hear, we can create new ideas and be more innovative.

In the end, making time for the quiet act of observation is an investment in ourselves. It feeds the soul, strengthens the mind, and builds resilience.

Here are some specific tips:

- **Meditate or practice deep breathing.** These practices calm the mind, reduce stress, and enhance relaxation.

- **Connect with nature.** Spending time outdoors helps you feel grounded and centered.

- **Do some gratitude exercises.** Practicing gratitude for the good things in your life helps shift perspective and build strength.

## 7. Complete a Task Right Away

Learning good time-management techniques that enable you to focus on the most critical things and stop you from getting pulled into less important activities will go a long way to helping you maintain your resilience. I have a friend who is very successful in her business. I always see her traveling on Instagram, and you'd never know that she is juggling a very high-profile portfolio of clients. When I watch her work, I see that she answers questions and produces deliverables as soon as they come across her desk—she's never got a pile of work waiting for her or something she's shuffled to the bottom of the pile. By doing this, my friend can free up large blocks of time and manage her schedule to include lots of personal travel. By handling things quickly and efficiently, she never has fires to put out or lapses in communication.

Finishing your work as soon as possible has many advantages. It keeps you from accumulating things to do and feeling overwhelmed, keeps you in the driver's seat and moving forward, and keeps you producing at the highest level. You'll be more efficient, you'll check more items off your list, you'll feel more in control of your work, and you'll feel a real sense of achievement from getting stuff done. This will in turn motivate you to feel good about yourself, move on, and take on more.

Here are some specific tips:

- **Be a time-management pro.** Effective time management prevents feeling overwhelmed and reduces stress.

- **Outsource where possible.** Don't be afraid to ask others to do things for you. It will free up your time and energy so you can focus on the bigger things.

- **Learn to say no.** Setting boundaries is essential for preventing burnout and maintaining balance.

## Conclusion

A strong work ethic is less about putting in the hours than it is about the mindset that underpins them—the attitude of diligence and conscientiousness that goes into getting things done, accompanied by a steely determination to meet and even to overcome the odds in the pursuit of excellence. It is the resilience built over years of trying, failing, trying again, and trying harder, and the conviction that we can overcome obstacles that we, and others, might have once considered insurmountable.

A strong work ethic makes us more capable, more effective human beings inside and outside the workplace, giving us a sense of agency and control over the inevitable ups and downs of our lives.

The habits of discipline, persistence, and versatility required to make your hard work count also contribute to the resilience necessary for success in a changing world. If you come to understand that setbacks are inevitable but surmountable, you can also recognize the power of a strong work ethic to help you rise above adversity and find a more meaningful and fulfilling life.

# CHAPTER 4

# Agility

Just when you think you've got the world by the tail—that whatever you've built is going to last forever, whether it's a business, a relationship, your home, or your career—you may learn to your surprise that nothing lasts forever. That's when you put the resilience you've been banking to work. You pick yourself up, dust yourself off, and start all over again. And when you do that, you may find that the next thing you build is even better than what you lost.

Before I was fired from the SCLC, I had every reason to believe I was on a success path that would continue for years, if not decades, into the future. However, when that path was blocked, I quickly considered my options, tapping into my passions and the entrepreneurial things I had done during my life. This led me to zero in on my ability to build and nurture relationships with elected officials and policymakers, and it allowed me to take the risk of starting my lobbying firm.

And as I mentioned in the previous chapter, it wasn't easy—there were forty thousand registered lobbyists in D.C. at the time, and the competition was fierce. But I stayed agile and light on my feet, and I built a successful business in that industry after facing what could have been an insurmountable obstacle.

But, to my surprise, it wasn't meant to last.

One morning—a morning like any other, nothing special, nothing out of the ordinary—I received a call from my business partner's office. The gentleman on the other end of the line told me that my business partner no longer wanted to move forward with Perennial Strategy Group and Perennial Sports and Entertainment, and my staff and I had exactly twenty-four hours to vacate the premises.

What's striking is that my business partner and the man I called one of my best friends, whose family I spent holidays and vacations with and whose kids I watched grow up, to this day has never called me to discuss what happened. The loss of business was one thing; the loss of a brother stung much worse.

As you can imagine, that news hit me like a ton of bricks. But I didn't have time to sit and stew or head down to the Willard Hotel bar to drown my sorrows. I had a limited amount of time to shut down the business and get everyone and everything out of the office. I didn't even have time to put a plan together. I had to move quickly—right *now*—to ensure that I didn't lose the clients I had worked so hard to gain.

The transition to whatever new company I was going to start would have to be seamless—it would have to give the impression that this was just another phase in the growth of my business. And thus, the name Phase 2 Consulting.

Talk about the need to be agile—and resilient!

The first thing I did was find new office space, which fortunately was available in the form of a shared office space upstairs in the same building. That would ensure continuity of our physical location for our clients. Then I had to arrange for movers to get everything up to the new office. It was midnight before the movers arrived, and we literally moved *every-thing*—desks, chairs, filing cabinets, the whole works—up to that office in the middle of the night.

As my longtime assistant Elizabeth Thomas describes the scene: "I remember Lamell calling us into the boardroom to tell us that his partner had pulled out and that we were left to build a new business from scratch, literally overnight. We had to rename the company, rebrand, and do everything from getting a new tax ID number to setting up payroll to creating a new website and email address. These are things that you would prep months in advance for that we were literally having to go learn on our feet and do overnight."

For the most part, my clients never really knew what happened. I lost a small handful in the transition, but most of them stayed with me and my new lobbying firm. The name Phase 2 represented the resilience I brought to my new venture—it was the next logical step in my life and for my clients. Things had changed fundamentally, but there was continuity with the past. I'd spent the first phase of my life working for success. I was now moving to the second phase of working toward significance.

My experience goes to show that you have to be agile, and if there is a lot of emotion tied up in some event—like the one I was confronted with when the plug was pulled on Perennial Strategy Group—then you've got to quickly work through that emotion to get to the next step for continuity, for sanity, and to preserve your business. As Kent Matlock says, "I guess the lesson in resilience for Lamell was not to talk about it, but to be about it!"

Again, I could have gone down all sorts of pathways that wouldn't have allowed me to achieve my big-picture goals. I could have told my partner, "I'm not going anywhere—I'm calling my lawyer, and you can talk to him." I could have burned up a lot of time, a lot of capital, a lot of energy, and ended up in the same place—a closed business. Frankly, I didn't have the time or the resources to get caught up in a protracted legal battle. But even if I had taken that path, I might have lost all my clients and ended up with nothing. Instead, I acted quickly and was able to salvage my business—albeit in a completely different form than I ever expected.

I was in shock, but I did what I needed to survive. And I did it by drawing from my deep well of resilience and being agile and decisive.

Part of agility is understanding that a difficult change like the one I went through with my business doesn't always have to be negative. Sometimes change is positive, and knowing how to quickly assess the situation and put yourself in a better position than before can be a real opportunity for long-term success. You may not soar immediately, but it's really about sustainability—it's about getting your footing back.

And it's about understanding and having faith that God has a way of turning things around for your good. I am reminded of Romans 8:28—coming to understand the fact that all things work together for the good—and its relevance for our lives even as I write this book! When now I step back and look at the big picture, I realize that the loss of Perennial Strategy Group and Perennial Sports and Entertainment was probably one of the best things that could have happened to me. Ultimately, agility is recognizing the good that's going to come and focusing on the positive outcomes that await you.

## The Power of Agility

All of us know that life is a complicated thing, but it's also an experience like no other, paved with a near-endless succession of joys, sorrows, challenges, and triumphs. To navigate with grace and resilience this complex life that God has given us requires a unique skill: *agility*. It's the ability to adapt, pivot, and find new paths when the old ones are blocked. Agility isn't about merely surviving life's storms—it's about thriving in their midst. And it's a key habit in your resilience code.

Imagine for a moment that you're considering a career change. Perhaps you've spent years building a successful career in one field only to find it disrupted by economic shifts or personal aspirations to do something that's more fulfilling to you. This can be a daunting, even terrifying, prospect. But for people who possess agility, it's an opportunity for reinvention. It requires courage, of course, to take that first step into the unknown. But it also demands flexibility, a willingness to learn new skills, and a relentless pursuit of knowledge.

This is where agility shines. It's the ability to see the change not as a threat, but as a chance to explore new opportunities. It's about redefining success, setting new goals, and building a different kind of life. It's about trusting your instincts, even when the path forward is unclear.

Agility isn't just about big life changes though. It's also about the small adjustments we make every day. It's about how we respond to unexpected challenges, how we handle conflicts, and how we navigate the complexities of this fast-moving modern world in which we live today. It's about finding balance between work and personal life, ambition and well-being.

Cultivating agility is an ongoing journey that starts with self-awareness. Understanding our strengths, weaknesses, and values is essential for making informed decisions. Mindfulness helps us stay grounded and focused, allowing us to respond to challenges with clarity. A growth mindset is indispensable because, instead of mistakenly believing that we can't change ourselves—that what we are today is what we will always be—it fuels our belief in our ability to learn and grow. And ultimately, that's what life is all about: learning and growing as people.

Building a strong support network is also crucial. I have had the good fortune to build a tremendously powerful network of friends, family, business colleagues and clients, and others on whom I lean when I need help, and they know they can lean on me whenever the shoe is on the other foot. Surrounding ourselves with people who encourage and support us can make a world of difference. They offer a friendly ear, a shoulder to cry on, words of wisdom, and support when we're feeling down. In the face of adversity, their belief in us can be a vital lifeline that makes all the difference.

Agility is not about perfection. It's about progress. It's about learning from mistakes. It's about picking ourselves up and moving forward—in a completely different direction if need be. It's about embracing the unknown with courage and curiosity. Ultimately, agility is a powerful tool for creating a life that is not just ordinary but *extraordinary*.

Agility is often associated with the business world, where it refers to an organization's ability to adapt to market changes. However, the concept is equally applicable to individuals. Personal agility is the ability to do the following:

- **Think flexibly.** Challenge assumptions, consider multiple perspectives, and find creative solutions.

- **Act decisively.** Make quick, informed decisions even under pressure.

- **Learn continuously.** Embrace new information, skills, and experiences.

- **Recover quickly.** Bounce back from setbacks and failures.

Resilience and agility are intertwined. Agility is a key component of resilience, enabling individuals to adapt to challenges and find new ways forward. Conversely, resilience strengthens agility by building the mental and emotional fortitude needed to embrace change. As we all know, perhaps some of us all too well, change is something we can always count on to happen—whether we like it or not.

Here's how agility contributes to personal resilience:

- **Enhanced adaptability.** Agile individuals are more comfortable with change and can pivot quickly when faced with new circumstances.

- **Increased problem-solving ability.** Agility fosters creative thinking, enabling people to find innovative solutions to challenges.

- **Improved emotional regulation.** The ability to adapt to changing situations helps individuals manage stress and emotions effectively.

- **Greater self-efficacy.** Agile people are more confident in their ability to handle challenges, which boosts their overall resilience. It's a virtuous cycle that continues to build as people gain increasingly more confidence.

The benefits of agility are far-reaching. Agility can enhance your career prospects; make you a more effective leader, team member, or worker; improve your relationships; and contribute to your overall well-being. For example, an agile employee is more likely to thrive in a dynamic workplace, while an agile parent can better manage the challenges of raising children.

Ultimately, agility is a powerful tool for building personal resilience. By cultivating flexibility, adaptability, and a growth mindset, individuals can navigate life's challenges with greater ease and confidence. It's an investment in yourself that yields significant, long-term returns in terms of personal and professional success.

## Ana Diego and the Power of Resilience

Ana Diego is a remarkable young woman from Mexico who now lives in Atlanta. Life has thrown her some immense challenges, especially after losing her mother in a tragic hit-and-run car accident. Despite the heartache, Ana has taken on the role of caregiver for all five of her siblings—showing tremendous agility in making the shift from daughter and sibling to the head of her household. Her ability to be agile deepened Ana's well of resilience.

Says Ana, "I'm trying to do my best to raise them and be a better person. I don't know what is going to come after for them, but I want them to know that I love them, that I want everything good for them. I want them to have a better life than my mom."

Her love and dedication to her family are truly inspiring, and it was a privilege to offer Ana a bit of help during my Twenty-Two Days of Gratitude, though her courage and determination are what truly shine. I keep her in my thoughts as she continues this challenging journey.

## Seven Ways to Be Agile and Increase Your Resilience

In today's fast-paced and ever-changing world, the ability to be agile and resilient is essential for coping with the demands of everyday life. Agility allows you to react and bend to whatever comes at you, while resilience enables you to pick up the pieces and recover from the adversity and setbacks all of us must deal with from time to time. Developing these twin pillars of agility and resilience is the key to achieving increased success in all areas of life. Here are seven potent strategies for developing agility, which will build resilience.

## 1. Don't Be Afraid to Change Course Mid-Stream

When it became clear that Perennial Strategy Group was to be no more, I could have kicked and screamed and held on for dear life—as the ship sank and me with it. And believe me, the thought crossed my mind more than a few times. But what I ultimately decided was that I would be wasting my time, money, and energy doing that. The best course of action was for me to pivot to a new business, a new opportunity, and that became Phase 2.

Make no mistake about it. Pivoting to Phase 2 threw me out of my comfort zone and was a scary thing to do—Perennial Strategy Group had been my home, my foundation, my personal identity for sixteen years. But I knew I had to change course, let go, and forge ahead to the next opportunity.

Sometimes life just happens, and we need to be able to go with the flow. It's not always possible to plan every step of the way, because circumstances are constantly changing, and there's only so much we humans can control in the world around us. COVID-19 is just one example. No one expected it, and countless companies—particularly restaurants and other public-facing businesses—had to permanently close their doors as the disease forced us to remain inside our homes.

Be open to alternatives and redirection if you find that your vision has changed. If you aren't flexible and willing to change course, then any setback becomes a problem, and you don't have a way to cope. As an agile person, you will be able to strike a balance between tenacity and the ability to go with the flow—to make changes as you need to along the way.

Here are some specific tips:

- **Develop a growth mindset.** Having a growth mindset is the belief that your abilities can improve over time, even if you struggle with certain skills. This differs from having a fixed mindset, where you believe that your abilities are static and can't be changed. So, embrace a growth mindset where you view challenging situations as opportunities for learning, not failure.

- **View setbacks and failures as opportunities to learn and develop.** If you're a human being like all the rest of us, then you're going to experience setbacks and failures—they're just part of life. To counter these inevitable events, have a Plan A, a Plan B, and even a Plan C. Your Plan A might be the most important thing you can do, but that doesn't mean that you can't, or shouldn't, change it. Have a Plan B and a Plan C ready as backups and be prepared to quickly switch gears as the situation warrants.

- **Seek feedback.** Check in with yourself and others along the way to see how you're doing. Ask for feedback from managers, coaches, colleagues, mentors, or family and friends who can be constructive critics.

## 2. Don't Get Stuck in Analysis Paralysis

If you're thinking about making a decision, and it feels right, it's probably the right decision. I could have easily gone into analysis paralysis before I made the decision to start up Phase 2 Consulting, but I knew the best thing for me to do—the *right* thing for me to do—was to hang on to as many of my clients as I could and pivot to an entirely new business. I was still *me*—the same guy that these clients knew and trusted—and I felt certain that many would follow me wherever I went.

Analysis paralysis often comes from the natural fear of failing we have, along with the desire to get everything perfectly right. We want the perfect solution to our problem, so we spend months looking at the options, trying to learn more, thinking things through, getting backup opinions, and doing all the things we do to make sure we have made the correct choice. But by hesitating as we wait for all this input, we simply delay the decision we need to make—sometimes to our considerable detriment.

Being agile means that you are willing to make the best decision possible with the information you have available right now, then are willing to change that decision if more information comes along.

Here are some specific tips:

- **Set time limits.** Decide in advance how much time you will spend analyzing the decision so you don't get stuck in endless analysis. Give yourself a deadline for making a choice and stick to it.

- **Weigh the pros and cons.** Make a list of pros and cons so you can more clearly see the options arrayed before you. What are the advantages and disadvantages of each of the potential outcomes? How will each choice affect you or your team or organization in the future?

- **Practice making decisions.** As the old saying goes, practice makes perfect. Make lots of small decisions so you can learn the process of decision-making. Start with things that have low stakes and work your way up to more crucial ones.

## 3. Avoid Second-Guessing Yourself

Self-doubt is persistent and corrosive, and it can inflict irreversible damage on your confidence, your potential, and your journey through life. It can prevent you from being agile and ready to shift gears when you need to. In fact, just one moment of indecision can snowball into a series of second-guesses and what-ifs.

To be more agile and strengthen your resilience, you must eliminate—or at least minimize—that inner critic and trust your instincts. Rather than constantly replaying your decisions, you should learn from them. No matter the outcome—good, bad, or somewhere in between—each experience provides you with the opportunity to gain insight and knowledge about the person you are.

In many cases, self-doubt reflects a fear of failure or a sense that we are not good enough. It manifests in how we assess our capability against some other person—the rising star on the team, for example—and we may tend to be overly critical of ourselves. This can leave us with a sense of inadequacy. Remember that we all experience self-doubt; it's a normal part of our being. Regularly remind yourself that mistakes are an inevitable part of learning and growth and that you can identify the lessons in this experience that will help you to move forward in a more positive direction.

Here are some specific tips:

- **Celebrate successes.** Notice when you're doing things right, no matter how big or small, and reward yourself with words of praise. Take notice of what you're doing well and what your strengths are. Acknowledge when you've improved.

- **Be kind to yourself.** When things go wrong, try to offer yourself the same kindness you would a good friend.

- **Get support.** Call someone you trust—a friend, a counselor, or a mentor—and share your doubts. Your feelings can easily seem bigger to you than they are in reality. Sharing what's on your mind could change how you view what you're experiencing.

## 4. Challenge Your Beliefs

What we believe shapes our reality and creates our subjective world. It also impacts how we behave. And while it's essential to have a set of core values—our deepest set of beliefs about ourselves and the way we interact with the world around us—it's also essential to be willing to question assumptions. When our beliefs are too rigid, they narrow our perspective and constrain our potential to adapt. To develop agility, try to imagine looking at the same situation with different eyes and be willing to change your mind about what you see if experience tells you the evidence points to a different conclusion.

The assumptions you carry in your mind are in great part based on your past experience. And because they often set boundaries for thought, you must force yourself to see things in new ways. Seek out fresh perspectives from those who look at the world differently and do things differently than you do. Read books by authors of different backgrounds. Watch documentaries with opposing viewpoints. Debate with a coworker or your significant other. Watch people whose point of view is different from yours.

When you are faced with new information or ideas, try to see them as a genuine opportunity for growth—a chance to expand what you know and how you think about it. While it's normal to be reluctant to let go of long-held beliefs, are there specific points that make you think twice about the new information? Instead of outright rejecting something that differs from your own view, try asking questions and drawing out the reasoning behind the alternative. Where are the similarities? What is different? Does this alternative idea make sense?

The key is to *think different*, as the tagline from the Apple computer marketing campaign used to suggest. When you let go of your own certainty and give genuine consideration to the ideas of others, you are more open to thinking in flexible and creative ways—you're more agile, and you build resilience.

Here are some specific tips:

- **Be exposed to other views.** Read. Watch documentaries. Listen to podcasts. Talk with people from a variety of backgrounds and lived experiences. Immerse yourself in ideas that push the boundaries of your current beliefs.

- **Debate others.** Intentionally look for and entertain other perspectives that are counter to your current position and debate with those people who hold them—in a friendly but deliberate way. The nature of the topic isn't important; just find something you disagree on and may learn a new perspective from.

- **Be open to new experiences.** Be willing to experience new things and try new activities. Strive to encounter novelty or involve yourself in activities that might give you new perspectives. For most of us, there are a nearly infinite variety of things that are outside our comfort zone and daily habits to choose from.

## 5. Don't Be Limited by Popular Belief

How many times have you thought, *I'm too old, too slow, too late*, or whatever, and you've allowed it to slow you down—or stop you altogether—when you know you should be moving in a different direction? Unfortunately, we all tend to adopt these kinds of self-limited beliefs, and once we adopt them, they're really hard to let go of.

Agility and resilience are not a young person's game—we all have the ability to be more agile and more resilient if we want to. Indeed, the older and more experienced we become, the more resilience we may need to build if we're going to sustain a good life. But regardless, we can *all* benefit from building agility into our lives.

Society presents us with behaviors that are considered to be normal or acceptable. But succumbing to that kind of conformity deprives us of our individuality and genius, so I suggest that you dare to be different. Do what you think your passions are telling you to do and do it confidently and without hesitation. Be true to yourself and your unique identity.

Bucking the status quo takes confidence and courage, as well as the conviction to go against the grain, to forge your own way, even if others don't understand or approve of the direction you choose. Often the right track to happiness and success is your own, not the straight and narrow.

There will be hurdles along the way—including well-meaning naysayers who will try to stop you, push you back, and work against you as you diverge from your socially acceptable path. But if you have a network of people who believe in you, who are nurturing you, and who are encouraging and supporting you along the way, then you have a really good chance of realizing your goals and your dreams.

If you have the courage to live your life as your authentic self and be true to who you are, you not only stand a good chance of achieving your ultimate happiness, but you can also motivate other people who might be struggling to find a way to be themselves. By living as your true self, you will become a shining example to other people who may have their own problems finding a way through the mire of self-doubt.

Here are some specific tips:

- **Think about what matters to you.** Identify your values and live accordingly—act in a way that is congruent with your personal beliefs and goals.

- **Create a posse.** Surround yourself with people who encourage your uniqueness and believe in your goals. Seek out others who also believe in themselves, have the same values, and pursue similar life goals.

- **Don't listen to the noise.** Well-meaning people will try to influence your decisions. Inevitably, there will be naysayers who will shoot you down. However, the only person whose opinion really matters is you, and it's important to stick to your own path.

## 6. Surround Yourself with People from Different Circles

According to Stanford sociologist Mark Granovetter, "Your weak ties connect you to networks that are outside of your own circle. They give you information and ideas that you otherwise would not have gotten."[1] In other words, the loose and casual connections you have can be more beneficial than the strong ones because more casual connections are privy to information streams and ideas further outside your specific area of expertise.

We need diversity of thought if we want to learn and innovate and escape the echo chambers in our lives that are the result of our limited networks. Hang out with people who see the world differently, who are from different cultures and communities, and who think differently. Encourage them to share their world with you, ask probing questions, and reach out to them again when you're ready for more. Be curious. To enhance your agility, you need to empower others to speak up. Invite people into your circle who hold different beliefs and are willing to have honest conversations.

Diversity goes further than tolerance and far beyond multiculturalism. It is a constant curiosity and pursuit for the insights and understandings others have to offer. When speaking to people who have different views than your own, do it with curiosity. Ask questions so you really understand. Don't make assumptions or automatically judge others. Instead, be prepared to have your own views challenged. Your goal is to fill your life and your mind with the voices and ideas of people who live differently than you do, who think differently, and who see differently. Doing this will make you stronger and wiser.

Here are some specific tips:

- **Get involved in diverse groups.** Appreciate cultures that aren't your own by joining clubs, associations, or web forums that combine people from various backgrounds. Talk, share, and listen.

- **Travel.** Experience other cultures and perspectives. Get out of your house, your town, your state, and your country and open yourself to the experience. Wander and be changed.

- **Be open-minded.** Listen attentively and with interest to what others have to say. Seek to learn, broaden your knowledge, and demonstrate your willingness to do so.

## 7. Build Mind-Body Connection

As children, we run and move in all directions—up and down, left and right, spinning, arms flying. As we get older, our movements become more and more rigid and specific—sitting in a chair at work, walking through the aisles of the grocery store. If you ever spin in a circle, you put yourself in danger of throwing up. Expose your body to some new ways of moving. The point is that it's important to build a mind-body connection and then to constantly challenge it by doing things that "upset the apple cart."

One evening I was watching a women's flag football championship on TV with my girlfriend. The team that was winning was from Staten Island, New York. What most struck me was that the coach of this team never once got out of his seat on the sidelines. He was tremendously overweight, and I'm sure it was difficult for him to get up out of his chair. So there he sat for the duration of the championship. That was incredibly ironic to me. Here you had a group of women football players who were in shape, running all over the field, while their coach couldn't budge.

Creating a strong mind-body connection is fundamental to being agile. There is an interplay within us between physical health, psychological well-being, and spiritual aliveness. Mind and body are inextricably related, and damage to one will inevitably affect the other. Sufferers of stress and destructive emotions frequently display physical symptoms such as tension, exhaustion, or disease. On the other hand, neglect or illness of the body can manifest itself in mental and emotional decline such as anxiety, depression, or apathy—all of which can hobble your ability to be agile.

Here are some specific tips:

- **Get physical.** Find some form of physical activity you enjoy and make it part of your everyday life. Exercise, among other things, is beneficial as it releases endorphins, reduces stress, and promotes general well-being. And it makes you more agile physically and mentally.

- **Practice mindfulness and meditation.** Take time to cultivate mental clarity and reduce stress through mindfulness exercises. Focus on your breath and live in the now.

- **Take care of your body.** Eat healthy foods like fruit, vegetables, and whole grains (I have been completely plant-based for the past seventeen years). Good nutrition will help you feel good and stay healthy.

## Conclusion

Cultivating agility is a lifelong practice, not a one-time event. It takes dedication, self-awareness, honesty, and a willingness to change and grow. If you practice the strategies in this chapter, you will build an array of skills that will help you deal with the highs and lows of life more skillfully and flexibly.

Bear in mind that obstacles and setbacks are bound to occur, but they also carry the potential for growth and transformation. Embrace the discomfort that comes from stretching yourself and trust that you'll be able to recover from the difficulties and come out on the other side as a stronger, wiser person. Surround yourself with a network of people who challenge and inspire you. Find mentors, friends, and colleagues who share the same values as you. Discuss, share ideas, and exchange lessons and experiences.

Most important, be true to yourself and live by your core values. Trust your passions. You have a unique set of strengths and talents. Think different. Be different. But as you strengthen your flexibility and tenacity, keep in mind that your experience is your own and that the direction you choose is about progress rather than perfection. So, celebrate your victories, take lessons from your setbacks, and move forward with humility and poise.

You aren't just becoming more nimble and able to recover from life's blows—you are also modeling behavior and encouraging others to become agile and resilient. You are setting an example and becoming a role model. Trust in the process and let yourself grow. When you move with agility and grit, whatever the future holds, you'll be more able to navigate it than ever before.

## CHAPTER 5

# Vulnerability

**B**uilding resilience in your life requires a daily practice of grounding yourself from within, and this—depending on what you like or what works for you—can take many forms. It can include meditation, prayer, exercise, connecting with pets or nature, yoga, music, chanting, cooking, gardening, swimming, golf, and on and on. The list is endless and completely based on personal preference. The only rules are it should be a rotation of things you practice daily that make you feel connected to the here and now in a way that calms and centers you.

Personally, I practice yoga. And while I'm no expert, I've never experienced two classes the same way. I'm in awe of the daily differences in my practice and how my body and mind respond.

In one recent class, while lying on a bolster on our backs, we were instructed to put our arms in a trident shape, or goalpost, arching our backs and completely opening our chests—and with that, our hearts—to the sky. The teacher warned that this might trigger intense emotions or be difficult to do, because opening your heart that tactically or physically is unusual and creates a deep sense of vulnerability.

I scoffed when she said this, but when I got into the pose and opened my heart to the sky, I was shocked at how vulnerable I felt, and I realized how much of the day we spend with our chests slightly concave, protecting our hearts, our emotions, and our vulnerabilities.

This was powerful stuff! And it can be for you, too.

## The Power of Vulnerability

Many of us make a practice of never letting the people around us see us sweat. Parents don't want their children to see them worrying about their family finances. Spouses don't want their partners to know their boss just gave them a bad performance appraisal and they're worried about losing their job. Salespeople don't want their clients to know that if they don't make just one more sale, they're going to miss out on a big end-of-year bonus.

At some point, we've all got to be vulnerable to family, friends, close allies, and others in our life—letting them know what's going on, the good and the bad. And that's tough, because when you present an outer façade of being successful and that everything is fine all the time, having to admit to the world that you've got big challenges in your life is particularly hard to do. But it's essential to be vulnerable because when you are, you express your essential humanity and invite others to step in and give you their support—which they often will.

I've personally had occasions over the last two decades when I've had to be vulnerable—when I've had some rough times in business—and I've had to reach out to folks. I've got to admit that it was a scary place for me to be because I naturally want to give the appearance that all is well and everything is fine to my friends and family, my clients and business colleagues, and the world. But sometimes it's not, and I feel like I've got to keep up that façade because everyone wants to go with a winner—someone who's always got their act together.

Getting to that point of vulnerability and all that it represents isn't easy for someone like me—someone who was raised to remain stoic and tough and seemingly unaffected by the ongoing challenges of life and business. However, when you do take down the walls and become vulnerable to others, it's a liberating experience. It's freeing because you discover there are people in your circle who won't judge you. They will still think highly of you, still do business with you—and even still love you. They'll recognize that you just need a little help, encouragement, and support.

In a culture that venerates strength, independence, and survival, we often leave vulnerability in the shadows. Yet it is here in the darkest realms of the human experience that we find the truest sources of resilience—our ability to withstand all that life throws at us, not being afraid or reluctant to reach out to one another, and to live with integrity and authenticity.

When we make the decision to present a flawless image of ourselves to the outside world, we're making ourselves and those around us less resilient. Vulnerability brings with it empathy, understanding, and support. When we allow others to see our struggles, fears, and insecurities, it gives others permission to do the same. This creates a foundation of community and interconnectedness that has been shown to be one of the key ingredients for resilience.

Furthermore, vulnerability is also very closely allied to self-compassion. When we accept our vulnerability and admit to our limitations and imperfections, we engage in a more caring, compassionate, and supportive internal dialogue. Self-compassion plays a central role in resilience, enabling us to interpret things like setbacks as human and challenging, rather than personal flaws.

In fact, if we could classify the number of things that get in the way of vulnerability, at the very top of the list would be fear—fear of rejection, fear of judgment, fear of seeming vulnerable (or, to use a different word, weak). As Brené Brown said in her 2010 TEDx talk, "Vulnerability is not weakness. It's our most accurate measurement of courage."[1] To show up whole, as we really are, with full-on presence and vulnerability instead of a shiny fake veneer of awesomeness. Getting there requires breaking through the fear that holds us back.

Fear of being inadequate expands and thrives when we believe we're not good enough in some way—when we believe that our own unacceptable flaws will prevent our ideals of love and belonging. Yet only when we're brave enough to explore these deeply hidden aspects of ourselves can we find the vulnerability to accept our own imperfections and the imperfections of others, and therefore the way toward empathy, love, and belonging. When we show up and allow ourselves to be seen, we learn that we aren't alone. We discover that others share the same insecurities we have, that others also are afraid to show their true selves.

In relationships, the same vulnerability that exposes us to possible harm also enables the growth of intimacy—letting another person see the real you, warts and all. When I'm willing to share the truest aspects of my being, I not only invite the other person's truest self in return, but I also invite my own trust and understanding of them. We each embrace vulnerability and, in doing so, we both prosper. Such is the stuff of intimacy—of deep relationship.

Vulnerability can also be an important part of good leadership and teamwork. Authentic leaders can admit and share their own mistakes; they don't blame others when they are at fault. They ask for feedback from team members and are vulnerable about their own struggles. This creates a psychologically safe environment where employees feel motivated to take risks and bring their whole and unique selves to the table. This openness builds trust and camaraderie, which helps with collaboration and problem-solving.

As former Texas governor Ann Richards once said, "Resilience is not a trait you're born with—it's a muscle you build." So, by going to the hard places in our lives, by allowing ourselves to be vulnerable, we are building the mindsets and habits that allow us to thrive. Ultimately, the practice of vulnerability is a daily exercise—a commitment to come forward with courage and authenticity, despite the unknown and the uncomfortable. This requires self-awareness, but most of all, it requires the understanding and acceptance that we can't ever—no matter how hard we try or how intensely we long for it—control everything that happens to us or around us.

It takes a risk to be vulnerable—to put ourselves out there, to be open to the possibility (even probability) of rejection . . . of not being seen as we wish to be seen. And yet the benefits are immeasurable. When we stay unseen or allow ourselves to be seen only in carefully controlled ways, we lose touch with our core resilience and strength, our full creative muscle, and our ability to connect with others.

To be vulnerable and remain deeply present and authentic in the face of fear, ambiguity, and risk requires courage—the courage to allow our fragility and humanity to be known in the very ways we most fear. And the courage to trust that it's not despite those feelings of vulnerability but because of them—that we find the greatest resilience, connection, and meaning in life.

## Seven Ways to Use Vulnerability to Increase Your Resilience

Paradoxically, being vulnerable can enhance resilience by enriching our self-awareness and by making us more honest in our relationships, more able to handle the stresses life throws at us, and more willing to pursue personal growth by leaning into discomfort and embracing our imperfections. Here are seven ways you can use vulnerability to increase your resilience.

### 1. Admit When You're Wrong

Admitting we're wrong—being vulnerable enough to realize that sometimes we get it wrong—is a superpower. It's a strength, and shifting our focus to see how it makes us stronger is a resilience strategy. I'm not talking about just admitting you're wrong, but also doing the work to see what happened and why.

Showing that you can admit to being wrong is an important step in personal growth and resilience. It's easy to get defensive when you make a mistake, and an overly defensive perspective can lead to a very unconnected and unproductive life. But admitting that you messed up is just the opposite. When you do, you're communicating humility, honesty, and a willingness to learn. You're communicating that you're human, that you make mistakes, and that you are committed to growth. This keeps your relationships—both personal and professional—healthy, and it also means you're not spending time having to justify or explain your error. It gives you permission to solve the problem and move on.

Yes, it can be hard to admit mistakes, especially in high-stakes environments or when ego is on the line, but the advantages far outweigh the short-term discomfort. In work environments, leaders who admit their mistakes set a powerful example for how to be transparent and accountable, and company culture can follow. In personal relationships, it can deepen connections and build trust when people are willing to acknowledge their shortcomings and be vulnerable. In fact, admitting mistakes is often a mark of strength and self-aware-ness. It takes courage to face your own shortcomings, but the ability to do so builds resilience.

Here are some specific tips:

- **Practice self-reflection.** Ask yourself what you did and why it didn't work out. Be genuinely honest with yourself about how you might have gone wrong—without pointing the finger at someone else or making excuses.

- **Focus on the lessons learned rather than dwelling on the error itself.** Don't linger on your errors; instead, think about what you can take from them. Learn from your experience and try to do better next time.

- **Seek feedback from others.** Ask some trusted friends, family members, colleagues, or mentors for their perspective on what is going on. This can give you access to a wider perspective of the situation.

## 2. Don't Hesitate to Apologize

A genuine apology is a powerful way of restoring and renewing relationships and fostering trust. It takes courage to admit you have hurt someone and take the blame for your actions, but the rewards can be significant. To apologize shows empathy—that you feel remorse and are trying to make restitution. An apology is an expression of emotions, not a self-forgiveness or a release from guilt. It's an expression of regret toward the person who was harmed, and this apology can pave the way to forgiveness, reconciliation, and new and strengthened relationships.

It's one thing to say, "I am sorry." It's another thing alto-gether to say and feel, "I'm sorry because of what I did to you. I can now see that I hurt you deeply or violated your sense of worth. I want to make amends." Sometimes hearing such a heartfelt apology can be deeply moving and transfor-mative—not only for the hearer but also for the person doing the apologizing.

Offering a vulnerable and humble apology that exposes your fears and flaws requires enormous courage and energy—values that are part and parcel of being attuned to your emotions and competent in managing them to enhance your relationships and your life. At work, it can defuse a tense situation, resolve an ongoing conflict, or provide a fresh start. At home, it can begin the rebuilding of a relationship.

We don't have to feel like a loser when we apologize. Far from showing weakness of character or a lack of self-esteem, sincere apologies demonstrate a strength of character and a willingness to accept personal responsibility for your actions.

Here are some specific tips:

- **Be specific about what you're apologizing for.** An apology should be specific about what you did wrong. Don't just say the words *I'm sorry* and leave it at that. Explain what you did and why it was wrong. You should address the impact your actions had upon the other person and how you can see that they've been affected. Don't try to minimize the impact of your actions or the other person's feelings.

- **Show genuine remorse.** Be remorseful and use impassioned language to express your regret and sadness over what has transpired. Show that you are sorry for your words or actions by voicing a clear intention to make amends—that is, to say (and show) you are ready to do what you can to put things right and regain the other person's trust.

- **Follow through with actions that demonstrate your sincerity.** When you do apologize, make good on it through action. Take concrete steps to show that you mean it. You might have to make amends, apologize in person, or even change your behavior so you don't repeat the offence.

## 3. Be Honest with Yourself

Being honest with yourself is the heart of vulnerability. Telling yourself something that isn't really true is the opposite of strength. Being vulnerable enough to tell yourself and others around you the truth strengthens your resilience and yields a variety of other dividends.

Self-awareness is a fundamental part of personal growth and resilience. It begins with being honest with yourself about who you are, including your strengths and weaknesses, thoughts and feelings. Many people avoid self-reflection because they fear what they might find. But fearing your vulnerable spots typically stems from an inability to stare directly at things you think might be a problem, and this makes you feel the need to get away from uncomfortable thoughts. However, you can't change something until you're willing to be aware of it.

Once you see something as a pattern, you can take action to change it. This level of self-knowledge requires you to be completely honest with yourself. Without it, you can't make good decisions, form authentic relationships, or live a fulfilling life.

You must be willing to face uncomfortable truths, to challenge the stories you tell yourself about why you do things and what you want. This process of getting real with yourself can be uncomfortable, but giving it the space to happen is essential for growth and resilience. It's about being able to accept the things about yourself you wish were not true (without coming down on yourself) and to celebrate your strengths without a false sense of hubris.

Self-honesty also allows you to speak authentically and be more open with yourself and others. Appreciate that it's a journey, not a destination. Regularly check in with yourself, process your experiences, and welcome feedback.

Here are some specific tips:

- **Set aside regular time for introspection and self-reflection.** You can learn a lot more about yourself if you set aside time to reflect on your thoughts and feelings, whether that's in a notebook, on your computer, or somewhere quiet, doing nothing much at all.

- **Be open to constructive criticism and seek feedback from trusted sources.** A receptiveness to feedback is necessary for climbing the mountain of self-improvement. Ask the people you trust for their input so you can identify where you can improve and hear from those you place your confidence in.

- **Embrace your imperfections as opportunities for growth and learning.** Like everyone else, you have flaws, and it's not productive to judge yourself for them. Thinking of imperfections in terms of opportunities makes you more inclined to overcome obstacles and learn new skills.

## 4. Have Faith in the Unknown

Life is unpredictable, and controlling everything can be a huge drain—as well as being completely ineffective. To be comfortable with uncertainty, you must have faith in God or in something bigger than yourself. You have to believe that it will all come out right, even when you can't see the way. You need to be able to trust that there is a plan and then let that trust keep you moving forward. You learn to bend, not break, to turn failure into learning, and to make lemonade when you've got lemons. Faith will make you a stronger person.

Faith in the unknown doesn't mean you just passively accept whatever comes your way. But it does mean you can tell yourself, "This will work out. I am confident I will be OK. Whatever comes next is something to get excited about, to learn from, and to discover." Once you have faith in the unknown, you are more likely to take risks—more willing to step out of your comfort zone, to pursue the things you are committed to.

Let's say you are undergoing a major life change, such as a divorce, the death of a loved one, or the loss of your job. During such times, when so much is out of your control and the road ahead isn't clear, if you have faith in the unknown, it can alleviate anxiety, create a resilient perspective, and help you stay focused on the possibilities rather than getting derailed by the perceived impediments. Because, after all, you believe that you can deal with whatever comes next, even if it's unknown.

Here are some specific tips:

- **Practice mindfulness and stay present in the moment.** Pay attention to the present moment by observing your breath, your sensations, and your thoughts without judgment or interpretation. Using mindfulness, we can reduce stress while improving our focus and well-being.

- **Cultivate trust and surrender to the normal flow of life.** Trusting that the universe will meet your needs is more about surrendering control than gaining it. Allowing a sense of uncertainty can lead to greater openness and acceptance, and this will foster greater resilience.

- **Understand that uncertainty is an opportunity for new possibilities.** Instead of seeing uncertainty as something to be wary of and protect yourself from, think of this state of flux as a challenge, as an opportunity to develop new potential and skills.

## 5. Be Vulnerable Enough to Care for Others

Being vulnerable and showing another person that you care puts you at risk, especially if they don't reciprocate. Even worse, when that person doesn't reciprocate, you may go as far as creating walls, so you don't ever have to be vulnerable with them again. However, I believe the benefits of being vulnerable enough to care for others far outweigh the risks.

I can't tell you how many people—even perfect strangers—I wish I could go back in time and really thank for a level of caring that they extended to me. Ultimately, a significant amount of the resilience I have today is the result of the generous and heartfelt acts of others, and I am doing everything I can to pay them forward.

To be vulnerable enough to care means that you're open to the ebb and flow of feelings about others' well-being—your care for others can be expressed in times of challenge, in times of celebration, or simply in the quality of your presence in the moment. When you care, you also build up a bank of reciprocal care that will support you in difficult times, adding depth to your well of resilience. To be open to care also means the capacity to be vulnerable enough to see others' humanity and forge a connection with them.

This doesn't have to be all or nothing—it isn't caring for others at the expense of yourself. In fact, setting clear boundaries is vital to having sustainable care for oneself and others. The potential for a virtuous cycle of giving and receiving is a powerful method of building resilience.

Here are some specific tips:

- **Set healthy boundaries to avoid burnout and maintain self-care.** You can limit and establish boundaries— even say no sometimes—when you feel yourself getting stretched too thin. You go in that direction now rather than exhaustively paying for it later. This is how you can run a business and still have a life.

- **Practice active listening and empathy.** If you listen to others and are attuned to their points of view in a manner that is both receptive and respectful of their voice, then you'll create mutually supportive connections with others and enhance the general supportive atmosphere of life.

- **Find ways to serve others that align with your values and passions.** Doing things that are aligned with your values and passions will make you feel that your life is worthwhile, meaningful, and connected to something greater than yourself. Your life will flourish and so will the lives of the people around you.

## 6. Be Vulnerable Enough to Make an Unpopular Decision

Sometimes you're forced to make unpopular decisions at work or in your personal life. It takes courage, but also stick-to-itiveness.

If you believe something is right and make an unpopular choice, you show strength, integrity, and a core ideal. Think it through, but ultimately be convinced of your decision and be prepared to face the criticism. This is one of the keys to developing personal and professional success.

This requires being vulnerable to make unpopular choices—in other words, to shun the easy option for the sake of best interest over the long term. It means having the resolve to make such decisions and stand by them to show you have confidence in your judgment—even if it means taking on or deflecting the criticisms that come your way.

Of course, this type of vulnerability can really pay off with leaders because they're often in situations where it's part of their responsibility to make unpopular decisions. If you can demonstrate that you have integrity in your commitment to your principles, then you're likely to gain the support of the people who work for you, even if they don't necessarily agree with you in the moment. It's critical to communicate the reasons for such decisions and the thought processes behind them.

It's not about making unpopular decisions because you think they're right for you; it's about having the strength to see what you believe others would do if they had your level of reflection and transparency. Unpopular decisions don't mean rudely deciding without respect for others' opinions or feelings, but rather having the mettle to do what you think is right even when it's uncomfortable to do so.

Here are some specific tips:

- **Gather all relevant information and consider multiple perspectives.** Make sure you have done your due diligence and have all the data, facts, and input from stakeholders before you make your decision. The more varied the perspectives and the fuller the picture of a situation, the better the decision is likely to be.

- **Communicate your reasoning clearly and transparently.** When you've made a decision, communicate the rationale behind it openly and honestly. Explain your thought process, the factors you considered, and how you arrived at your conclusion. Transparency builds trust and helps get others on board, even if they may not fully agree.

- **Be firm in your convictions but be open to feedback.** Have confidence in your choices and be willing to stand behind them. At the same time, be open to listening to feedback, concerns, and suggestions from others impacted by the decision. Be willing to adjust if you are presented with compelling new information or ideas that could improve the outcome.

## 7. Be Vulnerable Enough to Push a Little Bit Harder

Stepping out of your comfort zone leads to growth and resilience. It is frightening to try something that requires stretching beyond your usual behavior, but it is also more than worth the effort. You can develop new skills, extend your horizons, and increase your confidence. And don't forget that when you take on challenges, you will experience setbacks. The key is to find your own way through to the other side, and as you do, you'll become more resilient and confident in your capabilities.

This kind of vulnerability means that you have pushed yourself hard enough to be uncomfortable—hard enough to not be certain of the outcome. It looks a little like setting big goals and aiming for the stars and sometimes falling on your face. But you know that in the end, you'll be a better person than you were before, and that's worth the effort.

To push a little harder, you need to have a growth mindset—that is, to see yourself as capable of increasing your capabilities day after day. When you push yourself, you become stronger in ways you may never have known otherwise. However, don't push so hard that you burn out or cause others to burn out. Push just a little bit harder at the right moments and recover a bit in the others. Trust that over time, you will manage to keep increasing your boundaries and building resilience at the same time.

Here are some specific tips:

- **Set challenging but achievable goals that stretch your abilities.** If the goal isn't hard enough, you'll either lose interest or you'll breeze through without much effort, both of which are recipes for losing motivation. Goals that are difficult enough to be interesting and invigorating but not impossible are likely to keep you engaged enough to actually attain them.

- **Break big goals down into smaller goals to build momentum.** Big goals can be intimidating, so break them down into a series of smaller goals. Accumulate a dozen small wins and you'll have the confidence and momentum you need to get the big goals done—one step at a time.

- **Celebrate your progress along the way.** Pause regularly to celebrate each win, no matter how small, so you can maintain your momentum and your motivation. Embrace a growth mindset and stay positive.

## Conclusion

Being vulnerable requires a commitment to be present, to be honest, and to know yourself. What are you afraid of? What drives your reactions? Why? All the answers are within you. It isn't easy to be self-aware. It can hurt to talk about your insecurities and uncertainties. But the truth, raw and honest, will set you free. With more self-awareness comes the ability to be present and act in a clear and focused way.

Vulnerability requires us to be courageous. When we are vulnerable, we risk rejection, and we allow our real selves to be seen by others. We often confuse vulnerability with weakness, yet it is simply the birthplace of courage. This is the place where we choose to become ourselves by showing up, letting ourselves be seen and truly known by others. It takes vulnerability to connect, to truly know and be known. It takes courage to do that. When we live and love with the courage and compassion to be vulnerable, we will be transformed into our true selves.

But resilience—the thing that helps us bounce back from adversity—is the cumulative result of venturing into vulnerability. By immersing ourselves in vulnerability, disappointment, and failure, we build our capacity for resilience. The more often we pass through it, the more likely we are to foster our capacity to endure it. Our experience of vulnerability is the environment out of which our resilience grows.

It's important to remember that vulnerability is not a destination; it's a journey. You will stumble and falter at times. You might lose your way and want to run back to the shelter of your comfort zones. But with each step you take, you will develop more compassion for your imperfections, more acceptance of your humanness. And in doing so, you build your resilience all along the way.

## CHAPTER 6

# Network

I think it almost goes without saying that there is a lot of power in our networks—the connections we have with others at work, school, church, and life. And you just never know when someone in your network is going to help you in a time of need or provide you with an opportunity when you least expect it.

When I was a student at Morehouse College, I was a religion major, and my favorite instructor was Dr. Aaron Parker, a religion professor who also pastored at Zion Hill Baptist Church in Atlanta. I became a student minister at Zion Hill, and I worked there my entire four years of college.

While I was in college, there was a gentleman at the church—a deacon, trustee, and alumnus of Morehouse who also sang in the choir. He also happened to be an NBA referee. In the early 1990s, you didn't necessarily see a lot of Black referees, particularly ones you knew and went to church with. I thought it was really cool that a guy I would see on television officiating games was at my church as a deacon, a trustee, and singing in the choir. And so, he became a big brother to me. We became very close over the years.

After I graduated from Morehouse and left to attend graduate school at the Princeton Theological Seminary, we kept in
touch. He was often traveling around the country to officiate
games, and sometimes we'd meet up if our schedules coincided,
or he'd leave game tickets for me. We stayed in contact from
when I was in college to when I started up my D.C. lobbying
firm in 2004. He didn't necessarily understand what my firm
did, but we were still close friends.

One day in 2004, he called and said, "Hey, man, I'm on
the board of the National Basketball Referees Association—
our union—and we've got to respond to the NBA regarding
a pay increase. We've got sixty-something referees all over the
country, and we've got to do it by silent ballot. I don't know
exactly what you're doing, but is this something that you and
your firm could facilitate?"

When you're an entrepreneur, you of course say yes to a
question like that and then you hang up the phone and figure
out how you're going to do it. In this case, it meant sending a
lot of FedEx envelopes to NBA refs across the country.

But as it turned out, stepping up and saying yes to this
task offered by someone in my network—an individual I
had met at church when I was a freshman in college—led to
everything I later did in sports, starting with a new business:
Perennial Sports and Entertainment. And it was all because of
the consistent outreach to my friend and consistently staying
in touch. Because of this connection, my firm eventually took
over responsibility for collective bargaining for every NBA
official nationwide.

Today, I tell my team that we spend so much time in business looking for outside opportunities that we often forget to
explore the opportunities that are right there inside our current circle of relationships. Is there a client who can help you
get another client? Can one of your friends, relatives, or other

acquaintances help you achieve a goal you've set for yourself instead of having to find someone new to provide the support you need?

In my own career and life, there were clients who helped me get other clients and members of groups and organizations I joined who helped me get the additional business I needed to sustain my growth.

When I speak to young people, I often say, "Show me your friends, and I'll show you your future." I can tell a lot about you if you show me your last five texts and/or phone calls! I'll show you your network—and your network can sometimes illustrate your potential net worth. Take some time every day to nurture and grow your network; when you do that, both your opportunities and your resilience will increase exponentially. In this chapter, I show you how.

## The Power of Your Network

Here's another story about meeting someone in my own life who led me to all sorts of interesting places, building my resilience all along the way. I met Martin Luther King III—the son of Dr. Martin Luther King Jr.—when I was a high school student living in Chicago. I invited him to visit my high school for a Black History Month program, and I stayed in contact with him over the years. When I graduated the following year, I went to Morehouse College in Atlanta, which is where he resided.

I remember seeing Martin on a college trip to New York City my freshman year. We were walking down opposite sides of the street in Times Square, and I yelled to him and called his name. He didn't recognize me at first, so I ran across the street to say hello. I'm sure he thought I was a crazy man! But it turned out that meeting him in high school, staying in contact over the years, and then bumping into him in New York resulted in a four-year internship in his office when he became a Fulton County commissioner.

I had a similar situation with Deval Patrick, who served as the first African American governor of Massachusetts from 2007 to 2015. I had reached out to him years before that when he was U.S. assistant attorney general during the Clinton administration. I was in graduate school, and I sent a note to him at the Department of Justice. My note went something like, "Hey, you're from Chicago, and I'm from Chicago. I'm a student at Princeton Theological Seminary, and I wanted to know if the next time I'm in Washington, I could come by and have a few minutes with you."

Lo and behold, Deval sent me a letter in response, and the next time I was in D.C., I was able to meet with him. And after our meeting, I made sure to keep in touch.

The one thing I've learned about building and maintaining a network is that you've got to put in the work. When you keep reaching out and keep relationships fresh, you cultivate a wide span of lifelong relationships that create a village—helping you lead and build resilience. These relationships give you advice and counsel and open up doors of opportunity for you—just as you open up doors of opportunity for others. There are literally people in my life today who have been in my network since I was a grammar school student.

With its intricate and fragile fibers, life is held together by a single strand: resilience. That ability to bounce back, weather the storm, and emerge from hardship stronger than before is what allows us to succeed through failure and seize opportunities when they land on our doorstep. And at the beating heart of resilience is one simple, powerful thing: *connection*.

The company we keep plays a pivotal role in determining whether we are prepared to weather life's inevitable storms. If things go wrong, having a group of people who continue to believe in us—through all the ups and the downs—can be just the inspiration, motivation, and revitalization we need to keep going.

Think of a young entrepreneur who has just failed in his first business venture. He is disheartened and in financial distress. However, if he has a supportive network of friends, family, and mentors who can give him a shoulder to cry on, advice for what he might do next, or even some financial help, he will be able to recover more quickly from his failure. He will be able to get up, dust himself off, and move forward again.

Diversity in our network increases our collective resilience. Having friends and colleagues from different industries, backgrounds, and lived experience exposes us to different knowledge and solutions for problems. This can help us find new solutions and enhance our adaptability. A diverse network can also provide us with the requisite resources and perspectives to cross unfamiliar terrain and respond effectively in the face of the unexpected.

Take the software engineer struggling to write a new application for her customers. She may need a graphic designer or a user experience expert to make the product more visually pleasing and easier to use. If she goes out to her diverse network of colleagues, this will enable her to escape the ubiquitous echo chambers entrenched in her team, helping her to see the world more broadly and in new ways.

Networking is a way to open yourself up to new possibilities. If you need a job, a partnership, or a collaborator, having a strong network provides a backup—a cushion for any disappointment or failure. A mentor or an expert in the industry can lend an ear and possibly provide you with a set of guidelines to follow, a road map for how to make your way—if not to the top, at least up the ladder a little.

A jobseeker could find employment through a network of peers. A writer might not be able to get their book published, but they could find a publisher more easily by collaborating with a successful writer. If I have an important question at work, I can ask one of my mentors or a successful individual in my firm.

Outside the professional sphere, resilience is also built through our personal social networks. Friends and coworkers can offer instrumental support and guidance while serving as a sounding board when times get tough, helping us to stay optimistic and grounded. Personal and professional networks can also serve as sources of empathy—we can support others who are facing stressful situations, and they can offer the same support to us. Knowing that others have been through the same ordeal can provide great reassurance.

When faced with a challenge or hardship, being able to talk to friends or family who can lend an ear, offer support and suggestions, and potentially share experiences is invaluable. Because if others have been through what you're going through, then you probably have a chance at seeing light at the end of the tunnel.

Another reason is that a good network might provide access to resources—information, skills, or social contacts that could be useful in addressing your challenges and solving your problems. This in turn may lead to shared resources and support from fellow network members (for example, helping with childcare or sharing a car) that could make it easier to deal with problems and enhance resilience.

For instance, a young entrepreneur who is having trouble drumming up capital might be able to make connections with investors or lenders. A student struggling to get through a challenging course could find a tutor or study group. Tapping into the resources that are made available through our networks helps us to both expand our chances of success and overcome obstacles to it.

Engaging with our networked community can also help us gain more skills and knowledge that we need to adapt in an ever-changing world. We can do this by attending networking events where we will be taught the skills we need to succeed in a world where everything is changing at an accelerated pace.

An individual who's looking for a career change, for example, could attend an industry conference or workshop to learn about new trends and technologies. A student who isn't sure what they want to do for a living might attend a networking event to get a sense of the career possibilities that most interest them. Investing in our professional development helps us to become more skilled and more resilient.

One thing to keep in mind as you build your network is that factors such as socioeconomic background, systemic barriers, and support systems significantly influence resilience, as follows:

- **Socioeconomic background.** People from lower socioeconomic backgrounds often lack access to resources, education, or healthcare that promotes resilience. They must work harder to build the networks many of us take for granted—or they may be excluded from them entirely.

- **Systemic barriers.** Discrimination and unequal opportunities, as well as institutional biases and prejudices, can hinder personal growth and coping opportunities, thus limiting resilience. We must all make an effort to stamp out discrimination when we see it and avoid the pervasive biases and prejudices that serve only to harm others rather than lift them up.

- **Support systems.** Family, friends, mentors, community organizations, and mental health resources provide emotional and practical support, serving as buffers against adversity and promoting resilience. Some of the most effective kinds of support systems include the following:

  » **Community resources**—local organizations offering support services, such as counseling and financial aid

  » **Educational programs**—access to training and skill development to empower individuals

  » **Social networks**—building relationships for emotional support and shared experiences

  » **Mental health services**—professional help to address trauma and develop coping strategies

  » **Peer support groups**—sharing experiences with those facing similar challenges to enhance resilience

Resilience is not an individual effort—as the saying goes, it takes a village. Resilience is cultivated and reinforced through connection. By developing a strong and diverse network of professional and personal relationships, you can develop a web of support that will see you through the hard times—as well as the good—and emerge stronger than before. The people you surround yourself with can provide the inspiration, motivation, encouragement, and resources to move beyond the challenges and realize your goals.

## Victoria Pryson and the Power of Resilience

Victoria Pryson is a remarkable woman who has faced the harsh realities of homelessness but has triumphed through resilience and determination. Despite the challenges she encountered, she now stands tall in her new home, which she was able to purchase as a first-time homebuyer with the help of the I Am My Sister's Keeper Foundation in Ocala, Florida.

Sadly, people experiencing homelessness are often scorned and looked down upon by others, causing them to build very thick walls to avoid the pain and hurt. It takes real courage for these people to be vulnerable and open themselves up to individuals and organizations that want to help. Fortunately, Victoria has done just that, and her gratitude and resilience have grown as a result.

Says Victoria, "I really do appreciate the Foundation's generosity. For them to consider somebody else shows the character of God—to be so selfless and to give out of their heart and to give to somebody who they don't even know. Just know that it is not going unseen." Victoria is right—when you do good for others, it does not go unseen.

It was truly an honor to be able to provide her with some small but much-needed supplies and hear about her journey toward success. To Victoria and anyone facing obstacles, remember that perseverance, belief, and faith—and being vulnerable enough to allow others to provide their help and support—are the guiding lights that lead us back to stability. Keep pushing forward, for brighter days await on the other side.

## Seven Ways to Use Your Network to Increase Your Resilience

As we have seen, having a strong network can build your resilience in a variety of ways, including the ability to manage life's stresses and engage in the work of becoming our best selves.

When we lean into relationships for support and those who support us are there when we need them—and we're there when they need us—we can cultivate and sustain a sense of belonging and resilience that can aid us through life's challenges. Here are seven ways you can use your network to increase your resilience.

## 1. Don't Be Afraid to Reach Out to People and Stay in Touch

When it comes to professional networking, the most meaningful connections we have are the ones with the longest shelf lives. While many of us are quite excited to take on the latest networking opportunity, the best networking happens when we focus on the people with whom we've already connected.

Networking is a two-way street. Focusing on what you can get from your contacts is counterproductive, because others will not want to connect with you if your sole purpose is to ask for favors or advice. Stay in touch on a regular basis while offering value, and you will show the other person that you care about the relationship. This will make them more likely to support you in the future.

All it takes is a simple email, a quick phone call, or a coffee meeting to reinvigorate those ties. However you choose to do it, by making an effort to keep your connections alive, you are filling up a deep well of goodwill that can be useful in your personal and professional life.

The best way to lay the foundation of networking is to help others. Pass on a tip. Give frank and honest feedback, along with suggestions for improvement. Introduce people who might benefit from meeting one another. If you want others to give to *you* someday, be prepared to give to *them* today. When you help and support the people in your network, you increase the likelihood they will help you down the road.

The best-utilized network is the one you aren't only turning to when you need something—the best-utilized network is the one you've been working on slowly and surely. When you keep in touch and give as much as you receive, you'll find you've built a set of strong, long-lasting relationships—which, as I've pointed out, can be of tremendous benefit for all involved.

Here are some specific tips:

- **Stay in touch regularly.** Check in with your contacts every week, month, quarter—whatever works for you and your network. You need to put in the effort to keep these connections going, even if it means just a few minutes of your time each day.

- **Offer value.** If you read an article, see an industry news story, or find any other resource you think someone in your contact list at any level would find interesting, send it to them. A valuable truism when it comes to networking is that you'll go as far as you take others.

- **Celebrate their wins.** Congratulate your contacts on their promotions, career milestones, and more. A sincere and timely pat on the back goes a long way.

## 2. Make a Point to Leverage a Secondary Network

While the people in your primary network are critically important, don't overlook friends of friends, acquaintances, and others in your secondary network: the people in your second and third rings. These folks have perspectives and access to information you don't, and that can be very helpful for you—broadening your network of ideas and contacts.

An effective way to use your secondary network is to attend industry events and conferences. Take advantage of them, meet new people, and learn about what's new. Talk with people who have similar interests and make the effort to see where that can take you. Another approach is to use social media, such as LinkedIn. Make connections with people in your field, join groups, and comment on posts—this is an easy way to make connections you may not have otherwise.

And don't forget about the people you know who know you—you have the potential to reaffirm their regard for you and get access to new opportunities if you put some effort into these relationships. Ask the people in your primary network for referrals to the people in their primary networks and continue to expand your own primary network.

Here are some specific tips:

- **Tap your social media.** If you are hoping to get in front of hiring managers and decision-makers, LinkedIn and other social media platforms are a great place to start. If you don't have many connections, focus on expanding your network and your reach. Be an active poster and commenter on social media.

- **Find online communities.** Hang out in forums, groups, and discussion boards related to your interests. Chat and share what you know.

- **Hit the trade show circuit.** Meet people at conferences, workshops, and meetups. You can also host your own meetup.

## 3. Don't Feel Like You're Bothering Someone If You're Following Up

Following up is an essential part of networking. Don't worry if you don't hear back right away. People are busy. Sometimes they forget. Sometimes they simply need a reminder. There's a difference between being persistent and being a pain. Just because someone doesn't answer the first time doesn't mean you shouldn't try a second or a third time!

There can be merit in being a little bit persistent—if you follow up nicely—to emphasize the fact that you're serious about pursuing something. But you don't want to be a nuisance either. One of the main rules of persistence is if you've followed up four times and you haven't gotten a response, you're probably barking up the wrong tree. You might need to change course or pivot.

When you do follow up, respect the other person's time by not sending too many messages too quickly; you also can offer to provide some additional information or a reason for why you are following up. After all, persistence is one of the best networking skills you can have—politely and repeatedly following up is a great way to show that you're serious about a relationship and to finally get a response.

Here are some specific tips:

- **Be prompt.** Get back in touch soon after your initial meeting (within a week or two). People's memories are short.

- **Add value.** Supply some extra information or rationale for your follow-up. Make it clear you're not just sending a canned message you send to everyone.

- **Persist, but politely.** If the other person doesn't respond right away, follow up politely with persistent notes. But also pay attention to the other person's schedule and don't become a pest.

## 4. Give as Much as You Get

The most effective kind of networking is reciprocal, and the best way to build relationships with others that are mutually rewarding is to give as much value as you seek to receive. Give your time, your knowledge, and your network. Share news, offer advice, and make introductions. In giving, you're showing your commitment to the networking community and strengthening your chances of getting help when you need it. You reap what you sow.

Offer value by being a mentor or a mentee—experience and knowledge are powerful forms of capital, and sharing them is as rewarding for you as it is for the other person. It can build the foundation of a deep, long-lasting relationship. Another way to give back is to volunteer to a group or organization you care about. In this way, you can meet like-minded people and give back to your wider community.

Remember, the skill of relationship-building is about giving as much as it is about getting. Offer information as much as you ask for it—networking is a two-way street. By giving something of value, you create a support network that can give back to you in ways you never expect.

Here are some specific tips:

- **Be a mentor.** Mentor a junior colleague or join a mentorship program—either in your organization or in your community.

- **Volunteer.** Donate your time and talents to causes you care about. Giving back to your community can be very fulfilling and can also help you find people with similar interests.

- **Participate in networking events.** Organize and/or attend networking events for people in your industry. Look for opportunities to bring people together and form new relationships.

## 5. Practice Talking with Strangers

Few people are good at striking up conversations with strangers. But if you're looking to network, it's one of the most important skills you can cultivate. Every day, talk to someone new—the barista at your favorite coffee shop or the person sitting next to you on the subway. Make small talk and ease into real conversation, and you will find that you're able to warm up to new people just like anyone else. Everyone is a little nervous when they first meet someone and are afraid of breaking the ice.

One way to help people get talking is by posing open-ended questions, which tend to elicit longer and more interesting answers. Another suggestion is to be a good listener. Show genuine interest in what someone else says and avoid cutting them off. By listening, you demonstrate that you value their point of view and want to communicate with them.

Keep in mind that like any other skill, you can get better at this if you practice it. If you're really bad at starting conversations, try doing it more often. It will improve your self-confidence and your ability to build relationships. You'll find that those new acquaintances can quickly become friends and part of your ever-expanding network.

Don't be embarrassed to stand in front of the mirror at home and have a conversation with yourself. This is a great way to work at getting comfortable with small talk and approaching strangers.

Here are some specific tips:

- **Ask open-ended questions.** Keep your questions open-ended to keep the conversation going and let the other person lead. Instead of asking questions that can be answered with a simple yes or no ("Do you like your job?"), ask an open-ended question ("What do you like about your job?") to keep the conversation going.

- **Pay attention.** Make others feel heard by showing an interest in what they have to say, not just by creating a personal monologue. Pay attention to what they are saying, don't interrupt them, and don't drift off to some other thought.

- **Be an active listener.** Repeat what the other person is saying to rephrase their words and prove that you're paying attention and are interested in the conversation.

## 6. Hone Your Elevator Pitch

Your elevator pitch is your one-minute, memorable, and engaging narrative that summarizes who you are, what you do, and what you're hoping to find. Make it clear, concise, and catchy. Practice your elevator pitch until you can present it with confidence and ease. Expect to be asked about your background, experience, and goals. The more you know about yourself and what you want, the more ready you'll be to express yourself and to make the right connections.

When crafting your elevator pitch, focus on your unique value proposition. What makes you stand out from the rest of the pack? What do you bring to the table that no one else can?

Just remember, your elevator pitch is merely a hook that's meant to get people interested in talking to you. It's not a sales pitch, so make sure you're being your genuine self and coming across with your own personality.

The more you hone your elevator pitch and adapt it to different audiences, the greater your chances of landing on the right one. Have answers ready for questions about what you do and what you're interested in.

Here are some specific tips:

- **Get your pitch down.** Practice your elevator pitch until you're comfortable with the words and really believe what you're saying. The more you practice, the more natural your pitch will sound.

- **Make it flexible.** Adapt your pitch to different audiences and situations. Think of whom you're talking to, what interests them, and where they're coming from.

- **Be confident.** Convince yourself that you can do it and let everyone hear your enthusiasm. Others will believe you if *you* do.

## 7. Take Notes

If you're meeting someone new, write a few notes about the conversation. Capture their name, contact info, a summary of what you talked about, and action items you'll follow up on. This will help you remember what happened and keep it all straight. When you take notes, you convey your appreciation for the relationship, show that you're taking it seriously, and communicate that you want to keep it alive.

You might also consider using a contact management system to organize your network. Both of these actions will assist you in building and maintaining a network to support your next job move or find a new job altogether.

Remember, your network is your net worth. If you take the time to organize your contacts and follow up periodically with your network, you'll enhance your future possibilities. When you meet someone, write a little debrief in your notes about who they were, what you talked about, and why and when you should reconnect with them.

Here are some specific tips:

- **Use a contact management system.** Evernote, Salesforce, and Microsoft Outlook all offer ways of keeping contacts and contact information organized. A contact management system will make it easy to find the information you need and get in touch with people if and when you need to.

- **Take notes.** Jot down names, phone numbers, topics of discussion, and so on to help with recall and follow-ups.

- **Follow up.** Use your notes to send timely follow-up emails or messages. Following up promptly demonstrates that you're organized and serious about developing relationships.

## Conclusion

The old saying that your network is your net worth is truer today than ever before. As we've seen in this chapter, the people we already know are our great untapped resource. Our ability to achieve our goals can be greatly helped by the support and open doors that come from the strong relationships we have, if we just learn to ask.

Whether it's through the contacts of existing clients or the access to resources of friends and family, your network can be a powerful resource. Your own future can be a mirror of the company you keep. Be deliberate in building and maintaining those ties, and who knows what can happen?

Think of all the narratives of people who have managed to accomplish incredible feats by effectively utilizing their networks. Entrepreneurs have started lucrative businesses aided by friendly mentors. Job seekers have gotten their dream jobs through referrals from colleagues. Artists have found their audiences by connecting with others. We are nothing without relationships.

I know it's true, because some of my most amazing opportunities in business and life have come to me through my own network. And in turn, I've made a point of providing opportunities to the people in my network. Not because I have to, but because I want them to enjoy all the success in the world.

Look inward as you work to build your own self-awareness but also look outward as you build relationships with others. Invest in the people around you. Experience more. Reach out to cultivate new relationships. Not only will this make you a better leader, but it will also make you a more fulfilled individual.

CHAPTER 7

# Focus

Father Richard Tolliver was the rector of St. Edmund's Episcopal Church in the neighborhood where I grew up in Chicago. When I was in my twenties, he told me, "Lamell, if you're not careful, people will look at you and call you a gadfly." I didn't know what the heck that was, so I asked him what he meant. "That means you're here, there, and everywhere. At some point, you have to sit down and demonstrate that you can build something."

When you're presented with a great opportunity or facing a big challenge—whether in business, personal, or otherwise—the immediate reaction is to just be all over the place. It's like playing Whack-a-Mole. But the secret to success is to focus all your energy on one thing—one goal—until you succeed at it. Know a lot about one thing instead of knowing a little bit about a lot of things—work on one goal at a time instead of spreading yourself too thin.

Focus on what's most important, and you will succeed. It may not happen overnight, but with focus, it *will* happen.

## The Power of Focus

Focus is an increasingly scarce resource in our hyper-connected social environment. Especially in today's world of information overload and noise, staying focused is not only beneficial, but vital to resilience, achievement, and mental health. This heightened ability to focus can form a cornerstone of creating the power and flexibility to overcome the obstacles in life and grasp the opportunities that arrive on your doorstep.

Focus is, fundamentally, a muscle that's strengthened with repetition. If physical training makes you stronger, mental practice builds your brain power. With each bit of sustained effort, your powers of sustained attention expand, and you become better able to maintain your rationality when both the good stuff and the bad stuff come. There are many benefits to this increased mental sharpness, such as a boost in problem-solving skills, attention to the present moment, and the capacity to respond carefully instead of impulsively to life.

A clearheaded mind is your own kind of North Star, guiding you through the unknown. Whenever barriers get in your way, or unexpected circumstances threaten to throw you off course, a singular focus on your goal will keep you going. And this commitment, sustained with focused attention, makes the difficulty turn into an intermediate step toward your ends. You can see clearly, be on track to reach the big picture, and carry forward even when you are disappointed with your short-term success.

Growing in a growth mindset—the belief that we can learn and improve from our experiences—has an all-important connection with focus and resilience. This approach reimagines the experience of adversity as a challenge to be embraced rather than a defeat to be shunned. It is in deliberately concentrating on the self and the potential that we establish a self-fulfilling prophecy of resilience. It's an attitude that allows us to look for obstacles, see failure as a chance to evolve, and live life in the future—not stuck in the past.

Concentrating on your life helps you to become more efficient so you can get the most out of your finite time, energy, and focus. When you focus on what is most important, you reduce energy wasted on irrelevant worries or activities. That specificity of squandering helps to have buffers in the event of critical circumstances. Concentration, devoting fewer resources to unnecessary tasks, and accumulating a reserve of mental and emotional resources are all advantages of such focus.

A narrow focus on your life also encourages learning flexibility, allowing you to digest new information, adapt to a dynamic environment, and implement knowledge in new ways. This psychological adaptability is one of the building blocks of resilience, as you can quickly bounce back from defeats and use failure as a learning experience. You become more flexible and resilient if you fully embrace new experiences and challenges, hone your capacity to change views in a flash, and use what you learn in new situations.

Focusing your attention can also help to balance stress and maintain well-being. By bringing attention to the here and now through meditation or mindfulness, you can wake up your body's relaxation mechanism and counteract the harmful impacts of long-term stress. The results of this disciplined stress management include better physical health, emotional stability, and greater adaptation to life's bumps and bruises.

As a problem solver, particularly in times of crisis, you can use the clarity of mind that comes from concentration. Rather than succumb to reactivity or decision paralysis, the enlightened mind is capable of extracting information, considering possible alternatives, and making decisions based on longer-term objectives and principles. This kind of enlightened decision-making is an essential feature of the resilient person and helps them make better decisions in the face of a crisis and to maintain a sense of agency.

Putting attention on the good things in life—success, gratitude, love—helps create a bank of positive emotions to sustain us in times of need. Such practice of intentional positive action doesn't entail being ignorant about challenges but is a means to see them from a positive and solution-based perspective. These are the fruits of this positive focus—greater hope and resilience, stronger interpersonal connections, and more social support systems.

The relationship between attention and resilience fosters cognitive flexibility, the capacity to switch between modes of thinking and modify mental tactics as circumstances require. This mental agility is essential for thinking holistically about challenging issues and quickly shifting gears if the first solutions don't pan out. Through prolonged concentration, being open to information and insight, and cultivating stability and agility, we acquire this vital intellectual flexibility.

Clear attention helps you better know yourself and become more aware of what is happening to you. This elevated self-awareness is an important resilience factor, helping to identify stressors early and take proactive steps to stay healthy. Meditation, frequent monitoring of your emotions, and cultivating a set of emotional strategies are all excellent techniques for building emotional intelligence with attention.

Leaders who focus their attention on their priorities and objectives set a strong example for their people to follow. By cutting through the noise and ensuring that everything stays sharp through the chaos, clearheaded leaders can steer their teams in uncertain times, develop resilient company culture, and improve performance and team harmony. This leadership clarity is essential to the growth of strong team relationships and organizational performance.

When our attention tends to drift due to constant contact with the many digital devices and diversions in our lives—from instant messages and email to the steady ping of social media on our smartphones—staying focused is extremely valuable. People who manage to focus while faced with digital distractions are better at processing information, problem-solving, and getting things done. Developing digital resilience means cultivating intentional interaction with technology, developing tools to deal with overload, and maintaining the right amount of both online and offline activities.

Attention works in ways that go beyond immediate returns, contributing a cascade effect that enriches all parts of our lives. Focused practice speeds up learning and perfection, focused relationships increase connections and comprehension, and focused self-reflection provides meaningful long-term growth. Long story short, focusing attention on the important stuff in your career and business is likely to result in professional success. Focus leads to moments of insight and innovation.

Developing focus can be an everlasting source of resilience in a world that constantly seeks to break it. When we cultivate a higher capacity for ongoing attention, we gain a powerful tool for how to deal with life, opportunities, and personal development. Focus allows us to solve problems in a timely manner, handle stress well, make wise choices, and remain resilient when the going gets tough—whether the challenges are for positive or negative reasons.

Focus develops our learning responsiveness, cognitive adaptability, and emotional intelligence—all elements of resilience in our dynamic, rapidly changing world. By continually developing focus, we build not just our own resilience, but also that of our teams, organizations, and communities. This is the essence of the power of focus—a building block for a more durable, flexible, and fulfilling existence, where we can thrive in any environment and make the most of whatever opportunity or challenge may arrive.

## Tony Plunkett and the Power of Resilience

Tony Plunkett is a single dad in the Atlanta area whose wife of thirteen years unexpectedly passed away in July 2021 while giving birth to their third son. Since then, Tony has been working fifty-five hours a week to try to keep up with his bills—all while being a single parent. It's a tremendously difficult spot for Tony to be in, but through his hard work, he has built and sustained a solid foundation of resilience so he and his boys can thrive.

Says Tony, "I try to do everything as much as I can myself—I try to do everything I can to keep their lives as normal as possible. But at the same time, I work as much as I can to be completely self-sufficient and support them."

In addition, Tony knows the power of gratitude, and his gratitude further fuels his resilience in the face of some very challenging times. As Tony explains, "I admire people who take the time and to give back to other people. . . . Even the simplest things mean a great deal. I appreciate everything that anybody's done for me. A lot of people have stepped up and been very generous since I lost my wife. I appreciate all of them."

It was an absolute pleasure to personally meet Tony during my Twenty-Two Days of Gratitude, and I am truly grateful that I was able to help him out a bit on his journey.

## Seven Ways to Use Focus to Increase Your Resilience

For some people, one of the most elusive things they can do is the very act of focusing. It can be extremely difficult; for some people, the attempt to focus results in a torrent of ideas and thoughts not organized in any particular way from all corners of the mind. This mental explosion of thoughts and ideas makes it extremely important to learn how to prune or weed out information that shouldn't be there.

The good news is that there are solutions to this challenging situation. By learning how to prune or weed out distractions and information that don't belong—that take you down the wrong track—you can develop a clearer, more focused mind. Here are seven ways you can use focus to increase your resilience.

## 1. Focus on One Thing at a Time

With so many things to do in such a short time, it's easy to feel stressed and overwhelmed. And while the desire to multitask is understandable, this habit invariably leads to less productivity and more stress. The trick is to focus on one thing at a time.

The more we try to do things at the same time, the more scattered our brains and the shorter our attention spans. We may feel like we're getting a lot done, but in reality, we're just spreading ourselves too thin. However, by taking care to work on one thing at a time, we're giving that thing our full attention and getting much better results. We feel productive and sense our accomplishments more richly.

Single-tasking can be a real challenge, considering that our culture reinforces multitasking as a virtue, but the benefits are obvious. When we focus on one thing at a time, we are less likely to make mistakes. We are also more likely to get things done on schedule, without unnecessary stress and fatigue.

The most important difference between single-tasking and multitasking is that the environment for single-tasking must be optimal. That means no distractions—turn off your phone and your computer and find a quiet place. It also means practicing realistic goal setting and task decomposition.

Think about it this way: When you incorporate single-tasking into your life, you'll get more done in the same amount of time. You'll also experience less stress and feel a greater sense of accomplishment. If you're flooded with ideas, write them down, decide which one to do a deep dive on, and put the rest aside.

Here are some specific tips:

- **Create a conducive environment.** Turn off the phone, close unwanted internet tabs, and find a quiet place to work.

- **Divide big tasks into manageable chunks.** If you have a big task ahead of you, it can feel overwhelming and impossible to tackle. Break it down into smaller, more manageable chunks so it seems less terrifying.

- **Cultivate time-management skills.** Time blocking, the Pomodoro technique, and the Eisenhower matrix are great time-management skills that will help you maintain your focus and avoid burnout.

## 2. Set a Timer

It can be hard to find moments of quiet when there are coworkers, family members, pets, noise, and notifications forever clamoring for our attention. We know mindfulness is good for us—it can help us manage stress, improve focus, and boost our mood—and one of the simplest ways to develop mindfulness is to set a timer.

Picture yourself sitting at a desk, surrounded by stacks of paper and a computer screen. Your mind feels jumpy and unfocused. You're having trouble deciding what to work on next, and your concentration levels are low. You might feel at a loss for what to do, but instead of surrendering to that negative state of mind, take a deep breath and set a timer for five minutes.

When the timer starts, close your eyes and turn your attention to your breathing. Breathe in, feeling the air fill your lungs. Breathe out, feeling your body relax. Notice how your body feels as you sit in your chair. Notice the coolness of the air on your skin. Notice the warmth of the chair on your body. If you can, let go of whatever thoughts are running through your mind.

When the timer chimes, spend a minute or two taking stock of how you feel. Are you more relaxed? Clearer? It's amazing what five minutes of concentrated attention to your mindfulness can do.

If you find this difficult at first, you can gradually increase the length of your mindfulness sessions and try different techniques, such as a body scan or a guided meditation. Find what works for you and make it a habit in your daily life.

Using a timer can be a powerful way to help you practice mindfulness, giving you a framework to focus and let go over a set period of time. Next time you're feeling stressed, take a breath and set a timer. Give yourself the gift of a moment of peace.

Here are some specific tips:

- **Expand on the mindfulness technique.** Most people find it helpful to set a timer to go off after a certain time and use that as a signal to return to the present moment. But there are lots of other tools you can try to bring yourself back—for example, the body scan meditation, as follows.

- **Do a body scan meditation.** Begin by getting comfortable in a sitting or lying-down position and then turn your attention to your breath as it moves in and out. Once you feel grounded, start to move your attention slowly through your body from head to toe, noticing any sensations such as tension, warmth, or coolness. If your mind wanders, gently bring it back to your body.

- **Try a mindful eating meditation.** This approach involves paying attention to the experience of eating—the appearance and smell of the food, the taste and texture. When you slow down and savor each bite, you can create more space and presence and deepen your relationship with your food.

## 3. Decide on What Kind of Stimulation You Need to Focus

There has always been a debate on what environment is best for concentration. Some say that being in a noisy environment helps them concentrate better, while others say that they need complete silence in order to focus well. Others are somewhere in between. The truth is that it all depends on your personal preference and also on your brain chemistry.

Studies show that noise can function as both a distractor and a stimulant. For example, low-level background noise, such as the sound of quiet rainfall or cafe chatter, has the potential to be a useful type of white noise—masking potential distractions. In other words, it has the potential to be a good kind of noise for people who are easily startled by a sudden or unexpected sound. On the other hand, too much noise can be overstimulating and detract from one's ability to think.

The "Goldilocks" level of noise for concentration might also depend on the nature of the task. A moderate level of noise could be helpful when it comes to creative or other problem-solving tasks, while deep concentration and attention to detail might require complete silence.

Of course, what works best for you depends on your own individual preferences and tolerances. The best way to know whether you should work in noise or silence is to try both and see. Experiment with focusing in different environments and pay attention to what works for you. Some people find that they need different levels of noise and silence throughout the day, depending on the task they're trying to do.

In the end, what makes for good focus is a workspace that works for you, whether that's a coffee shop, a quiet library, or somewhere in between. Find what works for you and own it.

Here are some specific tips:

- **Experiment with different noise levels.** Try to work in places with varying levels of noise. Do you prefer working in perfect silence, moderate background noise, or a bustling environment?

- **Find your sound.** What types of noise work for you? Nature sounds? Ambient music? White noise? Find the sounds that help you focus and remove perceived distractions.

- **Tailor the noise to your own environment.** Use technology to create your own customized noise environment. There are many apps and tools that let you mix and match the sounds you hear.

## 4. Not All Focusing Has to Be Done at a Desk

It's a myth that being productive is all about offices with white-washed walls, cubicles, and desks. While a quiet workspace might be one method of engaging in cognitive tasks, it certainly isn't the only one. Some of our brightest ideas happen in the most unlikely of settings when we find ourselves in a position to think freely and draw lateral connections.

Just think of the positive effects of a walk outside. Its natural rhythm, breeze, and changing landscapes can make you think in different and creative ways. Studies have shown that walking stimulates creativity, reduces stress, and lifts your mood. As you walk through nature, the dynamics of your brain changes, especially if you are not completely absorbed in your thoughts.

Similarly, the shower is a great place for thinking about and solving problems. Water's warm temperature and pleasing sound help relax you. The shower is a quiet place, devoid of distractions and interruptions. Without a clear focus, your mind is free to wander, making remote associations and generating creative ideas.

The trick is to be open to unorthodox work settings. Some people work best when they're on the move—others when they're sitting still. Try out different surroundings and see how you feel.

It's also worthwhile to allow for the possibility that not all productive work needs to be goal-directed. There's immense value in simply exploring, in indulging in low-energy, unfocused daydreaming and "staring into space"—all of which can lead to insights and breakthroughs that might otherwise have remained invisible if you were locked into a more laser-like focus on a particular task. Be open to how your brain processes information.

Here are some specific tips:

- **Designate a thinking space.** Find a corner of your home or a favorite place outdoors in nature that you can retreat to for recreation, reflection, and daydreaming.

- **Add movement to your day.** Take a daily walk, do yoga, or engage in other physical activities to stimulate your mind and body.

- **Mindfulness and meditation.** If you feel overwhelmed or uncreative, step back for a moment and engage in mindfulness exercises or meditation. These will help you stay on task and calm down.

## 5. Take a Break

The human mind is a great tool, capable of incredible creative and productive feats, but like any machine, it runs best after some downtime and a recharge. Knowing when to take a break is an essential skill for any productive person.

Most of us have encountered this familiar experience: We are struggling away at something, our attention focused intently on the task at hand, when suddenly we hit a wall. Our mind goes blank. We lose the thread of our thoughts, we can barely focus or concentrate, and our motivation evaporates. "Time for a break," we tell ourselves.

When you work continuously without rest, you can begin to suffer. Your productivity can decline, your work can suffer, and your stress can increase. In the long run, chronic overwork can lead to health problems.

Fortunately, there are a variety of ways to recognize that it's time for a break. Can you tell that you're not working at your best? Are you feeling tired, achy, or grumpy? Do you have trouble focusing your attention? If so, it's probably time to back off and take a break.

An effective strategy is to set a timer for your work periods; this can help keep you on track and avoid drifting off course. When the timer chimes, you can take a short break—either to stretch your body, get some fresh air, or just rest. When you do pause, make sure your activity is calming and restorative— walking outdoors, listening to music, meditating, or spending time with family and friends. Avoid anything that is stressful or stimulating. Those kinds of activities will make it harder to refocus.

You'll appreciate that the duration of your pauses is up to you and your needs and tastes. Some people find that short pauses every twenty, thirty, or even fifty minutes are helpful, while others prefer longer pauses less frequently.

Just remember that stepping away is not a sign of weakness. It's a sign of skill and self-care. When you know it's time to step away from your work and you give your mind and body a rest and return to your work with more productivity, less stress, and better well-being, it's a sign that you're great at what you do. It all starts with knowing when you're hitting a wall and when you need to break focus.

Here are some specific tips:

- **Discover your own personal rhythm.** Try out a variety of work and break intervals to find one that works best for you.

- **Establish a soothing stop ritual.** Develop a stop ritual of things to do that will help you to calm down and re-center yourself. This might include going for a walk, listening to music, or doing some mindfulness exercises.

- **Set limits and practice self-care.** Refuse to take on more tasks when you're overcommitted; instead build in time for activities that restore your mental and physical well-being.

## 6. Be Kind to Yourself

The grind mindset, with its self-help rhetoric of hard work and ambition—the belief that with enough grit and determination, you can overcome any obstacle and do anything—has become a pervasive cultural phenomenon. But what happens when the grind becomes a source of stress and burnout? Truth be told, it often does.

Not everyone is meant to be an all-the-time hyperfocus machine—some of us are at our best when we're at a lower level of focus or when we break our focus from time to time to give our minds a rest. We know that work goes better when we allow our minds to ebb and flow. When we force ourselves into the focus phase, we can't work at our peak, and we get the added bonus of feeling overwhelmed.

Be easy on yourself and remember that your relationship to work, deadlines, and efficiency might just look a bit different than your coworkers', friends', and family's. Stop trying to adopt a grind mindset if that's not your thing and find the rhythm that works for you. Play around with what techniques and strategies work best for you so your work life is sustainable and enjoyable.

So, be realistic about your goals and expectations. Don't make yourself crazy by trying to do everything at once. Instead, break down your tasks into smaller, more manageable chunks. This will help you to be organized and in control, and it will keep you from becoming overwhelmed.

Keep in mind that progress is never a straight line—you will have ups and downs, wins and setbacks. Be patient with yourself as you go along and celebrate your wins, no matter how small. If you are more compassionate about where you're at, you *will* get there. Find a rhythm that works for *you*, not for someone else. Be reasonable as you learn what type of focusing is most effective for you.

Here are some specific tips:

- **Recognize your natural rhythms.** If you are a morning person, schedule high-priority tasks accordingly. If you are more productive by late afternoon or at night, time your most important commitments to coincide.

- **Practice self-compassion.** Treat yourself with kindness and understanding, particularly when things don't go well. Say to yourself, "I'm having the normal reaction of being frustrated. I'm going to give myself a break and try again." Watch out for negative self-talk and give yourself pep talks instead.

- **Set small, realistic goals.** Instead of focusing on one large project and feeling completely overwhelmed, write down all the steps needed to complete the task, but break these down into smaller steps. By setting small, realistic goals, you'll be more likely to stay focused and feel motivated.

## 7. Keep Trying

The road to success is not a sprint; it's a marathon—a long-term, lifelong experience filled with victories and defeats. As you navigate the ups and downs of life, it's important to keep a watchful eye for what's working and what's not. What might have served you well in the past may not be as useful today. As the brain continues to grow and integrate new information, it sometimes benefits from a reexamination of the past. With this reexamination comes new opportunities and new ways to overcome the types of challenges that once seemed impossible.

In short, persistence is an undeniably powerful force. By trying and trying again, you signal your commitment to your ambitions and your faith in your ability to succeed. By attending carefully, testing and measuring your progress, and adjusting your approach when needed, you can clear the hurdles, learn from your mistakes, and realize your dreams.

The path to any worthwhile goal will be long and winding, but every step of the way, you will get closer to your destination. So, take the long road, trusting that if you persevere in adversity and keep trying, you will reach the mountaintop of your ambitions.

Here are some specific tips:

- **Set yourself up for success.** Minimize distractions and find a quiet space to work without interruptions.

- **Set realistic goals.** Do not set yourself up for failure by setting overly big goals or goals that are too unrealistic for you to attain. Instead, make sure your goals are achievable by breaking big ones down into smaller ones.

- **Take advantage of time-management tools.** Try out different approaches to productivity—the Pomodoro technique, time blocking, and others—to see what works best for your personal workflow.

## Conclusion

The words of Father Richard Tolliver have stayed with me for many years: "You're here, there, and everywhere. At some point, you have to sit down and demonstrate that you can build something." It was his way of encouraging me to set a goal and then focus on it until I attained it. Embracing a frantic pace and zig-zag approach to life isn't necessarily the way to success, but focused activity and sticking to a single thing can be.

I have found that the most meaningful progress in my own life—both professionally and personally—comes from a deep commitment to a single, well-defined pursuit. By focusing my efforts, I come closer to the zone of excellence than I would have if I tried to do all sorts of projects at once. "Don't try to do too much!" can sound trite or simplistic, but I have found that success, however you define it, is about doing one thing very well, not about doing many things not so well.

In addition, a singularly focused objective can provide a source of direction and purpose that can be invaluable in the face of hardship. When things go awry or the going gets tough, it can be all too easy to get stuck in a whirlpool of disappointment and despair. However, by continuing to focus on the one thing that really matters to me, I have managed to maintain an objective perspective, and when the chips are down, this has kept me moving forward with a gleam in my eye and a smile on my face.

I'm certain this will work for you, too.

## CHAPTER 8

# Dogged Determination

I have a friend who is afraid of heights. She generally avoids escalators and certainly won't take one up more than a single flight. Most of the time she just finds the elevator, which is usually in some faraway corner, crowded, and slow, but my friend's fear of heights far outweighs her need for speed.

This friend of mine is also a *big* shopper—she loves a good deal and enjoys shopping in new cities. She was in Paris last summer—and summer in Paris means *sales*. She had exactly one hour to get her shopping done and make a mad dash to the station before her train left. Faced with limited time and lots of ground to cover, much of which would require her to take escalators in the department stores, what was she to do?

My friend could have allowed her intense fear of heights to force her to throw in the towel and be content with the bags of clothing she had already purchased, or she could put aside her fear and carry on.

And wouldn't you know it—my friend made her way up those escalators in the department stores, five flights up, and successfully completed her shopping mission. I was shocked when she told me this story, and I asked her how she did it.

"Lamell," she told me, "I fixed my eyes on the goal and never looked down."

Now, this is what I call *dogged determination*—pushing through obstacles you normally wouldn't find possible—and it is a key habit of your resilience code. So, how do you apply it in your life?

In the face of a hurdle, a challenge, or a loss, you have to make a determination to keep moving forward—that you won't give up no matter how difficult the situation is. It's just not an option.

However, it's important to understand I'm not saying that *failure* is not an option—we're all human, and we all fail from time to time. None of us is perfect, and we learn valuable lessons from failure. What I'm saying is that if you want to succeed, *giving up* is not an option—you can't throw in the towel and walk away from success when you're on the threshold of achieving it.

In this chapter, I explore how dogged determination has helped me achieve my goals in life and in business, and how anyone can achieve more—be more—by employing this strategy in their own life.

## The Power of Dogged Determination

One of the characteristics that can make you successful in your career, business, and life is dogged determination—that is, perseverance in the ever-changing world in which we live today. This relentless determination to keep moving forward toward your goals, regardless of the challenges in your way, is not only an attribute of the successful, but also something you can cultivate and use to become more resilient.

A vital component of dogged determination is resilience under pressure. It's the spark that pushes you on when the road gets long and rough. In business as in life, there will be setbacks—we all encounter them all the time. These can be financial failures, market failures, emotional uncertainties, or the unpredictability of life. This is when dogged determination becomes what distinguishes the winners from the losers.

A concept related to dogged determination is *grit*—the passion and perseverance to reach long-term goals. According to psychologist Angela Duckworth, who has worked extensively on the concept of grit, it's useful to consider what grit *isn't*. Says Duckworth:

> Grit isn't talent. Grit isn't luck. Grit isn't how intensely, for the moment, you want something. Instead, grit is about having what some researchers call an "ultimate concern"—a goal you care about so much that it organizes and gives meaning to almost everything you do. And grit is holding steadfast to that goal. Even when you fall down. Even when you screw up. Even when progress toward that goal is halting or slow. Talent and luck matter to success. But talent and luck are no guarantee of grit. And in the very long run, I think grit may matter as least as much, if not more.[1]

Duckworth believes that grit predicts achievement more strongly than IQ or talent. Gritty individuals are growth-oriented, and their abilities can be nurtured through hard work.

This is a fundamental attitude in business. It moves markets, technologies, and consumer tastes. Those who overcome challenges with grit and dogged determination view them as opportunities to change, evolve, and win. They know that every challenge they overcome is a learning, an art.

Look at Jeff Bezos and Amazon. When he started his company, at first it was focused only on selling books. Bezos was challenged with doubts as to whether online shopping was even possible, along with stiff competition from well-established brick-and-mortar bookstores. But his indefatigable drive and learning ability enabled Amazon to pivot and expand. From an online bookstore to one of the biggest and most varied businesses in the world—from e-commerce to cloud computing to artificial intelligence, and so on.

Perhaps the most dramatic effect of relentless effort is rekindling self-belief and hope. If someone continues in the face of an obstacle, they prove they can do so. The result is an affirming feedback loop—strength produces resilience, resilience enables us to leap over hurdles, and doing so breeds self-confidence.

This increased self-confidence is essential to survive hardship. When faced with big difficulties or failure, those with a healthy belief in themselves are more likely to keep their act together and keep pressing ahead.

Take the example of Oprah Winfrey. Born and raised in poverty and forced to deal with personal and professional challenges early in her career, Winfrey's determination and self-belief propelled her into one of the world's most influential media figures. Because she worked tirelessly through the hardships, she was successful in so many ways, and that helped to make her stronger.

It's an essential skill to be able to adapt in today's ever-changing business landscape. A stubborn drive is key to enabling this flexibility. Unexpected disruptions or transformations require people determined to adapt but not get stuck in the dark. This flexibility doesn't consist of sticking with a disastrous approach after it has served its purpose. Rather, it's sustaining the drive to succeed while being adaptive about the process. It's knowing how to move when needed, with the ultimate destination in mind.

Netflix is a textbook case of this flexibility in the face of change, brought about by relentless tenacity. Although Netflix was initially a highly successful DVD rental service, it was challenged as streaming technology became available and people started to use it. Rather than hold on to their original model to the very end, Netflix pivoted. They made the move to streaming and then eventually to developing original content. All this versatility, accompanied by a relentless desire to succeed, has seen Netflix prosper in an ever-changing world.

Putting in the work against the odds naturally produces critical thinking and problem-solving capabilities. In the face of obstacles, doggedly determined people don't simply give up, they look for ways to do things differently, think outside the box, and create new alternatives for overcoming the challenge.

This habit of problem-solving, over and over, strengthens the human capacity for looking at an issue in multiple ways. It's based on an attitude of curiosity and creativity, in which any challenge is a question to be solved, not a brick wall.

People who develop dogged determination learn how to keep their emotions in check, even when they're experiencing a bad day. They learn to be resilient in the face of delays or failures or negative emotions. This emotional resilience is important at home and at work, so when they're under stress they can keep their heads up and keep working toward their goals.

At its core, dogged determination promotes "don't quit" values. This is the key to success and long-term achievement. It's knowing that the key to success isn't to succeed instantly, but instead to consistently achieve success over time. This resilience is the difference between those who make it and those who don't. It's to persist when others give up—to accept defeat as temporary and not permanent.

Persistent drive is often taken to be a personal characteristic, but it also can be quite a social catalyst. People who are persistent in pursuit of their goals will naturally attract others with the same ideals and goals. In business, this can be translated into building productive teams and collaborations. When people on your team have this mentality, they can bounce back, celebrate when things work out, and breed a culture of resilience and perseverance.

In addition, bonds that are built on a basis of this sort of communal determination are usually more stable. The friendships and mutual admiration generated by challenging one another can form powerful relationships that withstand hardships of all kinds, as well as the passage of time.

Perhaps the greatest effect of dogged determination is in helping to empower other people. Seeing people who show uncompromising devotion in the face of difficulties can inspire others to push through their own struggles and develop their own deep well of resilience. For example, the determination of hardworking leaders provides a model for their people to emulate—it's contagious. And the resilience of leaders in the face of failure can motivate people to push beyond perceived boundaries and establish an environment of resilience and innovation for an organization.

Take Malala Yousafzai, the youngest Nobel Prize-winner (she was just seventeen years old). Her persistent struggle for girls' education despite the very real threats against her life inspired millions around the world. And her unwavering devotion to her cause has not only advanced her but has also inspired thousands of others to fight for their beliefs and continue through obstacles.

What dogged determination is ultimately good for is that it enables people to achieve their intentions. In business, personal growth, or anywhere else, hard work based on determination is what makes goals happen.

The completion of a goal—particularly one that was not easily achieved without much work and struggle—can play a very important role in determining your self-esteem and well-being. It makes you feel good about yourself, and it helps you believe you can make it through anything and get ahead.

What's more, chasing and completing objectives with determined focus yields skills and attitudes useful in any area of your life. Resilience, problem-solving skills, emotional regulation, and persistence learned along the way become instruments you can leverage as you address a variety of problems and find your way to new opportunities.

Dogged determination is not merely a personality characteristic—it is a tremendously powerful tool for building strength, achieving tasks, and motivating others. By cultivating this quality, you can become more resilient, more responsive to change, and more effective at problem-solving, and in the end, achieve your greatest goals. When life throws you curveballs, perseverance will become a catalyst for your success.

## Seven Ways to Use Dogged Determination to Increase Your Resilience

Dogged determination—the willpower to carry on despite obstacles—is one of the key habits for achievement in life and in business. In our fast-changing and volatile world, the drive for success can be fostered as a source of resilience and determination.

People with grit are the ones who stand strong in their beliefs and don't stop in the face of obstacles that get in their way. They realize that the road to success may be difficult and long and they must continue on, even when the journey gets tough. When you adopt this quality, you build up confidence in yourself and your problem-solving abilities and develop the psychological resilience to thrive in life's challenges.

Here are seven ways you can use dogged determinations to increase your resilience.

## 1. Focus on Your Big Goals

You can't do everything at once, so sorting out what the big goals are from the ones that aren't as pressing is a good first step. Think of dogged determination as turbo mode. You can't drive in turbo mode all the time—you'll burn out your engine. You have to use it sparingly, saving it for something you really want to achieve. So, setting priorities is key.

Setting a goal is essential for personal and professional development. With clear objectives, you can orient your energy and attention to getting things done that will matter. This will guide you in how to delegate, how to manage your projects, and how to stay motivated along the way. Once your objectives are clear, you have a process that tells you how to move forward and holds you accountable to yourself. That sense of direction can feel tremendously empowering, as it provides a direction and a sense of satisfaction.

Enthusiasm is a force that can move you toward achieving your big goals by igniting your energy and commitment. The more determined you are, the more likely you will get through the difficulties, continue to thrive, and remain dedicated to moving forward until you succeed. This inner power lets you overcome adversity, learn from failure, and push through hardship.

When you track your progress toward achieving your goals, you make it easier to recognize accomplishments and be accountable to yourself. That sense of accomplishment can be extraordinarily rewarding, as it will reassure you that you really are in control and encourage you to push onward. Additionally, goal setting will help you learn about time management, problem-solving, and decision-making skills.

Here are some specific tips:

- **Be specific and measurable.** State your goals and make them as precise and exact as possible. For example, "I will increase my sales 20 percent in the fourth quarter of this year."

- **Empower yourself with realistic goals.** Never set unachievable goals that will only serve to frustrate and demotivate you. Rather, set attainable goals that challenge but motivate you to keep going.

- **Decompose bigger goals into smaller steps.** Break down your big goals into smaller steps, and you'll be more motivated through every single step forward. Not only that, but you'll gain momentum and confidence in your skills.

## 2. Identify Obstacles, Then Go Around Them

When setting out to achieve big things, it may seem daunting—perhaps even impossible. What do you do then? In my own experience, I've found that it can pay off to knock out some easier tasks first and save your energy for the biggest challenges. This approach can help you remain inspired, build forward momentum, and develop new perspectives and solutions as you work through the easier tasks.

Take every goal or project on its own and think about what the potential stumbling blocks may be. Are there external dependencies, resources, or big learning curves? With a thorough grasp of the challenges you'll face, you can create realistic plans to avoid them and keep them at bay on your timeline.

Make it easier for yourself by getting things done that don't take too much effort. They could be a little bit smaller and more manageable, something you can get done in a short amount of time and without committing a lot of time or effort. If you do those things before your more challenging projects or as a way of taking a break, this will save you mental and physical energy to do more complex projects and avoid burnout or low motivation levels.

Just keep in mind that you do not want to avoid tough work altogether—you just want to do it smart, when you have the energy and the focus to take it on. With small wins, you can establish self-belief, drive, and a feeling of accomplishment. This approach will keep you motivated as you find ways to move past the obstacles in your way.

Here are some specific tips:

- **Consider external factors.** See if there are any external variables such as dependency, scarce resources, or unforeseeable events that might delay your progress. If so, devise contingency plans to alleviate their effects.

- **Predict potential problems.** With your prior experience, knowledge, and know-how, you can predict issues that may come up in the task or project and plan ahead to overcome them or minimize their impact on your timeline.

- **Get feedback and input.** Ask your colleagues, advisors, or peers how you could have an edge and listen to their feedback. When you seek feedback from a diverse group of people, you increase the chances that you'll see what problems you might not be thinking about and come up with better strategies.

### 3. Make a Plan

What will you need to leverage to get what you're looking for? What tools are in your toolbox, and what tools are missing? One of the most effective tools in your toolbox is a plan. As the saying goes, what gets planned gets done.

This process begins by having an idea of what you want the plan to be. What do you want to achieve? How would your business, your career, and your life look after that? A well-thought-out plan will be a great motivator and will help keep you on track as you try to envision the final outcome.

After you know what you want, you need to take stock of where you're at. What do you already know? What are your resources, and what are your strengths? Finding your own strengths will enable you to tap into them so you can achieve your plan.

Then, you have to take into consideration anything that can stand in your way. What might your challenges be in the process? What stands in your way to making progress toward achieving your objective? By foreseeing possible setbacks, you can create strategies to conquer them and remain on track.

Here are some specific tips:

- **Make your plan visual.** This could be a mind map, flow chart, timeline, or other graphic. A visual representation allows you to see at a glance what in your plan is most important and where something is lacking.

- **Invite others into your planning process.** You don't have to create your plan all by yourself; in fact, you shouldn't. Invite your coworkers, friends, family, or mentors to help you create your plan—providing their own ideas and feedback—and then ask them to keep you accountable.

- **Be open to changing the plan as needed.** Life is unpredictable, and things change all the time. To account for this, be flexible and adjust and change your plan as needed so it's still within your vision.

## 4. Leverage Your Networks

The people you know personally form the cornerstone of your professional network. Those core relationships are invaluable, and they provide you with guidance, opportunities, resources, and support. The secondary networks—your primary contacts' friends and associates—are richer than you know.

This is what Stanford sociologist Mark Granovetter's groundbreaking paper "The Strength of Weak Ties" emphasizes: the importance of secondary ties. The good (close friends and family) are important, he contends, but the weak (friends of friends) are often the richest in terms of insight and opportunities. These relationships allow you to get access to knowledge and experience you might not get outside of your immediate community.[2]

As Granovetter explains, "Your weak ties connect you to networks that are outside of your own circle. They give you information and ideas that you otherwise would not have gotten."[3]

The key to making the most out of weak ties is building your network. Be active in industry meetings, professional organizations, online communities, and other places where you can network with others. Connect, discuss, and provide advice. Remind yourself that you won't get instant gratification when you establish these relationships, but it's worth the investment.

A multifaceted network, involving different people from diverse backgrounds, industries, and experiences, can be rich in knowledge and perspectives. Connect with people who can expand your perspective and challenge your beliefs.

Here are some specific tips:

- **Stay connected.** Keep in contact with your contacts, even if it's just an occasional email or text message. Be in their lives and businesses to build your connections.

- **Seek referrals.** Don't be afraid to request that your network refer you to potential career-relevant partners. Tell them precisely what you hope to achieve and how the relationship can benefit you both.

- **Give back.** Give something back to those around you by helping, sharing information, and connecting them with possibilities. Accumulating a good track record of being a helpful and generous person will improve your relationships and increase your chances of receiving help in the future.

## 5. Fix Your Eye on the Prize

Human imagination is a remarkably powerful thing, able to produce highly complex mental models. When employed intentionally, these images can have an enormous impact on our thoughts, feelings, and actions. Visualization is a particularly potent technique that involves seeing yourself reaching your goal. You can use a mental movie of yourself being successful to hook into your subconscious and push yourself to take action toward that outcome.

When thinking about your success, you want to be specific and concrete. Use visualization cues that reinforce the idea of you successfully achieving your goals. For example, imagine yourself hiking through a dense forest and chopping away the branches impeding your progress to clear a path. Mental imagery is extremely powerful, and when you are being dog-gedly determined, visualizing physically propelling yourself through to the finish line can help you actually get there.

You are bound to face obstacles and hardships as you pursue your aspirations. With visualization, you can work around these challenges and mentally prepare yourself for what is coming. Now, imagine you face these challenges in the real world, discover solutions, and overcome the challenges. Once you see yourself winning through obstacles, you will gain confidence and strength, and it is more likely that you will achieve your objectives.

Here are some specific tips:

- **Find a quiet place.** To visualize your achievement, start by finding a quiet place free of distractions. Lie down or sit quietly, close your eyes, and breathe deeply. Relax your body and brain.

- **Add sensory details.** It's good to add as many sensory details as you can to your visualizations, so think about the things you see, hear, smell, taste, and feel while you reach your end goal. For example, if your goal is to cross some foreign country off your bucket list, picture the sounds of the cities you'll visit, the smell of the unique cuisine sold by street vendors, and the warmth of the sun on your face.

- **Practice regularly.** The more often you visualize, the more certain your success will be, so take a few minutes every day to imagine your achievement. Your visual imagery over time will be more powerful and more vivid when you do, and this will keep you motivated and focused on your objectives.

## 6. Embrace Your Fears

Fear is an inevitable human emotion, one that often stops us from accomplishing our goals. Fear can be a scary thing, and yet it's not your worst enemy. Instead, it's an incredible motivator if you can make peace with it. In a moment of fear, it's easier to push through it. But that only feeds the terror and stops you from expanding. So, notice your fear and what it's saying to you. Should you have prepared more? Did you take on too much? Have you neglected something important?

When you have the answer to where your fear comes from, you can start to confront it. Make sure to remember how good you are and the successes you've enjoyed in the past. Imagine breaking through the obstacle and reaching your desired destination. The more positive visualization you do, the less scared you'll be.

Your fear doesn't have to be totally dismissed, of course. It's learning to accept fear as normal and take it as a natural avenue to growth. Once you start confronting your fear, you will become resilient, confident, and better prepared to take the plunge toward what you want.

You have to learn to tell the difference between healthy fear and unhealthy fear. Healthy fear is the result of a physical threat—it's a completely normal and expected reaction as your mind and body prepare to take an action, such as running away as fast as you can. Unhealthy fear, however, is grounded in unreasonable assumptions or unpleasant previous experiences that may have no bearing on what you're doing today and tomorrow.

Taking the plunge into something unknown can be intimidating, but if you really want it, you've got to steel your nerves and go for it. As the saying goes, you have nothing to fear but fear itself. Don't allow fear to paralyze you—accept it, embrace it, and allow it to propel you forward.

Here are some specific tips:

- **Understand your fear's origin.** If you can identify the exact root of your fear, you'll be better able to address it.

- **Try to outrun your negative thoughts.** Replace negative self-talk with positive thoughts and visualizations.

- **Be mindful and relax.** Mindfulness will help you stay calm and at ease. This means keeping yourself in the present by way of exercises such as deep breathing, meditation, and yoga. These exercises and others like them will lessen your stress and help you relax.

## 7. Don't Be Shy

One of the most powerful ways to move toward your goal is to access your support system. When you are able to share your journey with friends and family, it can be very inspirational and motivating. If you disclose your goal, you build an audience of cheerleaders who can congratulate you when you hit your goal—or commiserate with you when you fall short. You can rely on this assistance to stay focused, persevere, and remain positive.

It's also important to keep in mind that by disclosing your goals, you aren't requesting praise or approval. Instead, it's about being in deeper touch with others and finding common ground. If you talk about your journey, you might find that other people had similar challenges or are going through the same thing. This can create an atmosphere of friendship and wisdom.

And remember, you have achieved your victory with every little step toward it. Honor the small wins, acknowledge your effort, and be gentle with yourself. Although you might not immediately achieve what you want to achieve, the process itself is a valuable learning experience that can help you develop as a person.

Here are some specific tips:

- **Be specific.** When sharing your intentions, make them as specific as possible so others can understand what is involved and respond in a more appropriate way.

- **Have a support group.** Find like-minded people who will provide support and guidance. This can be a circle of friends or coworkers, or an online community.

- **Motivate your milestones.** Even if what you accomplished is just a small step toward your goal, be happy with every milestone as you make it. Refuse to get discouraged and lose your positive thinking.

## Conclusion

The strength of dogged determination is not only in how it allows you to achieve your dreams, but also the kind of person you become along the way. With every challenge won, every win whether big or small, you become a stronger, more accomplished person. And the impact isn't just on you, but also on others around you—potentially becoming a catalyst for positive change in your organizations and communities.

Remember, dogged determination is not a talent that comes naturally to a handful of people; it's something that can be developed. By seeing challenges as possibilities for improvement, keeping our eye on the prize, and relentlessly striving toward our dreams, each one of us can do more, be more. We then not only improve the likelihood of reaching our aspirations, but we also acquire the resilience required to survive in a volatile world.

Keep in mind that when things go wrong, it's not a matter of taking the easy road. It's instead a matter of making sure you will push forward, regardless of how rough the road ahead gets. In this way, you will find the success you're looking for.

# CHAPTER 9

# Faith

Faith is a deeply personal construct, and when I write about it in this book, I do so in a way that honors the multiplicity of unique and sacred ways people employ faith in their day-to-day lives, regardless of religion, nationality, creed, or worldview. Faith is an immensely important thing, no matter how you use it or who or what you choose to have faith in. According to a recent Gallup survey, almost half of Americans (47 percent) consider themselves to be religious, while one-third (33 percent) say they are spiritual. Another 2 percent say they are both religious and spiritual.[1]

As a son of Chicago's Black church and former divinity school student, I deeply resonate with faith in God. As you read this chapter, do so through a framework that resonates with *you*, in accordance with who you thank when you open your eyes in the morning, what propels you to be your highest self, and what you commune with in your darkest hours.

When you realize that I'm not just quoting esoteric scriptures about keeping the faith and holding on even when you can't see it, then you'll understand what I'm talking about.

When you come to a sense of confidence about yourself and are able to look in the mirror and say that *you* are the substance that is hoped for—*you* are the living, breathing, walking example—then you'll understand what I'm talking about.

## What Is Faith?

One of my favorite verses in the Bible defines faith as "the substance of things hoped for, and the evidence of things not seen."[2] When you can believe in things—yourself, your dreams, your goals, and others—in spite of not being able to truly discern every detail of how these things will get done or when they'll get done, then you are on the road to faith, and you're building resilience all along the way.

I believe that the connection between faith and resilience takes place when you realize that *you* are the substance of things hoped for and the evidence of things not seen. In my own life, this is especially the case when I think about ancestors who would have never dreamed of seeing me or folks that look like me achieve what we have in our lives.

Dr. Samuel DeWitt Proctor is one of my favorite preachers and authors. He was senior pastor at Abyssinian Baptist Church in New York City. He served as head of the Peace Corps in Africa, was the fifth president of North Carolina Agricultural and Technical State University and was a mentor to Rev. Jesse Jackson. Dr. Proctor wrote *The Substance of Things Hoped for: A Memoir of African-American Faith*.[3] Reading this book helped me realize and crystallize this idea that *we* are the substance of things hoped for, the evidence of things not seen.

While you might think of faith as all those things you're trying to achieve in your life, all those hopes you have for the future, there's a higher level where you can look yourself in the mirror—in spite of your successes or pitfalls or down-falls—and say to yourself, "I am the definition of faith. I am the substance of things hoped for, and the evidence of things not seen."

The fact that you're still standing, the fact that you're still pushing forward; the fact that you have a family—or a community that you call family, the fact that you have a job or something that gives you sustenance, financially, emotionally, or otherwise; and that you have a place to call home is evidence that you are the substance of things hoped for and the evidence of things not seen. With each passing day, you have the opportunity to build a deep reservoir of faith using tools that a researcher or scientist might find difficult to quantify, yet something within you burns with remarkable brilliance and unperturbable confidence. You can't see the finish line and have no idea how or when you'll get there, but you know you will. That's resilience!

Faith, while often associated with religion, is a conviction, a belief, a compass, a bright candle that can guide you through the darkness of uncertainty and the unknown. Faith comes in many forms, and an important part of it in terms of resilience is the belief in yourself—the belief that you got this. Faith is the unshakeable belief that you have the power to conquer any challenge, weather any storm. It's the voice whispering to you in times of doubt to keep going because you are going to achieve what you set your mind to. Faith is when you think you're flying without a net but then realize *you are the net*!

Faith is commonly manifested as confidence in a higher power, something between you and your God, where you know you are being looked after and are not alone, even when you think you are. Faith tends to take the form of a link to a higher power outside of self-belief. It's the reassuring knowl-edge that there is a spirit keeping you alive, even when things get bleak. And this union—whether in prayer, meditation, or just solemn silence—is comforting. It's the knowledge that we're here on this earth for a reason, and we're filled with the faith that things are going to be OK.

Faith is trusting your own path through the tough times and also the times through which you glide. It's recognizing that life is a series of ups and downs, a roller-coaster ride that may sometimes leave you elated and sometimes leave you crushed. When you have faith, you can accept the losses and the gains, to see them as a part of the path on which you're traveling. It is trust that, together with a belief in your strength, can allow you to meet the challenges of life gracefully and with persistence.

Faith in yourself is a deep love, even when you aren't ready to love yourself or think you aren't worthy. Faith reminds you that you *are*. Having faith in yourself is not judgmental. It's knowing that you deserve to be happy and successful. In the face of evil, faith shows you that you are worthwhile, you can love, and you can be awesome. It's the kind of love that fills the heart with the vigor and the tenacity to pull yourself through.

## The Power of Faith

Imagine yourself facing a particularly difficult challenge—how do you get through it? How do you even *begin* to get through it? You start by building your confidence and self-worth. Repeat affirmations out loud—in the mirror when you're getting ready to go to work in the morning or in your car when you're driving home after a long day. Say: "You are strong, you are worthy; you are valuable; your hard work will bear fruit." By believing in yourself and in your own worth as you take on the struggles and doubts, you will find a path, and faith will light your way.

Faith is a burning light that casts out the darkness, a reassuring compass, a grounding force that keeps us moving forward. It's a comforting beacon, one that guides us out of the dark corners of life and gives us sense of purpose. It's a stabilizer, keeping us in the here and now and stopping us from succumbing to worry and doubt. Faith is a shield, a force field that bounces negativity and doubt away and shores up resilience. It protects us from the toxic people and circumstances that can crush our faith in ourselves and undermine our drive. When we grow our faith, we are able to ignore those who try to tear us down and focus on what we desire.

Above all else, faith is hope. It's the hope we will see a better day. Our ambition, our determination, and our courage are all powered by hope. It's the thing that makes us passionate, the thing that drives us—despite how bumpy the road may be. Hope gives us drive, and drive makes us resilient. And faith gives us wings to fly higher over our struggles, to remain hopeful in the darkest night.

Make no mistake about it, at its very heart, having faith is simple. It's a matter of giving yourself over to a higher power—to surrender yourself fully. Faith is building a connection to something larger, a passionate love and self-esteem, a survival kit, a kindred spirit. Faith gives us access to this abounding source of strength and courage and provides us with the resources we need to push through challenges, make decisions, and live with purpose. And whether our path is one of personal difficulty, social unrest, or even a global catastrophe, faith sustains us to persevere, to rejoice in the grief, and to bounce back stronger than before.

May we all have faith in ourselves to stand the constant waves of life with strength, hope, and the attitude to never give up.

## Lamont and the Power of Resilience

On Day Twenty-One of my Twenty-Two Days of Gratitude, I visited the Legacy Center in St. Louis, where I met Lamont, a remarkable sixteen-year-old who had been mowing the lawns of elderly people in his neighborhood. Lamont had been a troubled student at school, and unfortunately, his teachers and the school seemed to have given up on him. But what I discovered is that at the Legacy Center, where he goes, he is the complete opposite of troubled. He is incredibly motivated, eager to learn, and deeply committed to helping others, especially in his role assisting the younger children there. I also learned that not only does Lamont have a strong desire to help people in his community, but he recently registered an LLC to start up his own landscaping company.

Once I found that out, I knew exactly what I had to do. I went to Home Depot and bought Lamont his own lawnmower and leaf blower—I made sure they were electric so he wouldn't have to worry about buying gas. When I presented that lawnmower and blower to him, I've never had a teenager embrace me the way he did. It was the kind of embrace that said, "Thank you not just for these wonderful supplies, but for believing in me, believing in my dreams, and shining a light on the path I am walking through life."

This was a first for Lamont. As he explained to me, such belief and generosity just didn't exist where he came from. People didn't believe in you and your dreams, let alone provide such tangible support. What I think I did for him was to illuminate a beautiful light on his journey. This light, a light he had never seen before, now guides Lamont toward possibilities he once believed were far beyond his reach.

It was remarkable. I've never seen a young man so happy and so filled with gratitude. And I think Lamont was touched so deeply that it forever changed something in him that he may not even realize. My hope is that he will long remember this experience and pay it forward to others in his community and in his life. I'm convinced that someday Lamont will be a beautiful guiding light to someone else. And it's all because he will forever remember the impact my modest but heartfelt gesture made on him.

## Seven Ways to Use Faith to Increase Your Resilience

Faith is a powerful force that can transform your life and propel you toward personal growth and fulfillment. It's not just about religious beliefs, but a broader concept that encompasses trust in yourself, the universe, and the journey of life itself.

Here are seven ways you can use faith to increase your resilience.

### 1. Embrace Faith as a Concept

Fundamentally, faith is about trust—in yourself, in God, or in the workings of the universe. It's the deep-seated certainty that you can get through difficult challenges and that you're never ever on your own, even in the worst of times.

Blind trust sounds daunting to many. As a society, we demand empirical facts and tangible outcomes. But faith works differently. It's the muscle of tenacity, the one thing that propels us forward when facts and reason crumble under us.

To embrace faith, begin by accepting it in your day to day. Know that when you make a plan for the future, your faith is what bridges the gap between today and tomorrow. When you sit in a plane with confidence that the pilot and crew know what they're doing, you're exercising faith. With these little doses of faith in mind, you can also build up a deeper and more comprehensive faith in life's experience.

Faith is trust—trust in yourself, your God, the universe, the Divine. Putting blind trust in yourself or something bigger than you can be a challenge at times, but faith is truly the backbone of resilience. Cultivate and embrace it.

Here are some specific tips:

- **Keep a faith awareness journal.** Record the times during the course of your day when you felt you embraced faith, however small. Consider the impact these events had on your day.

- **Practice gratitude.** In the same journal, each night make a list of three things you're grateful for and consider the part that faith played in enabling those people and things to come into your life.

- **Recite affirmations of faith.** Create and repeat affirmations aloud every day that help you build faith in yourself and the universe. Say things like "I can overcome this challenge" or "I will succeed this time."

## 2. Give Yourself Time and Space to Grow and Cultivate Your Faith

Faith is not a one-and-done event. It's a lifelong process that takes time, commitment, and self-care. Don't get down on yourself for having doubt or not feeling certain, as these are natural stages of developing your faith. Instead, make small steps and adjustments along the way.

Spend time on a specific task each day to grow in your faith. That may be prayer, meditation, journaling, or even some silence. Keep in mind that the faith journey is your own. What works for others might not work for you, and that's OK. Wait for yourself to find the traditions and rites that are appropriate for your own personal spiritual journey, wherever it may take you.

Gaining faith won't happen overnight, especially if it's not something you lean into regularly. Give yourself time to grow your faith and notice the small changes in yourself and others along the way.

Here are some specific tips:

- **Create a faith growth map.** Draw a timeline of your faith journey, listing important moments and times when you've expanded it—or when it's been tested.

- **Design a sacred space.** Create a relaxing, sacred space in your home that is dedicated to your faith journey. Decorate it with meaningful objects and use it for reflection or meditation every day.

- **Build daily faith stories.** Create a daily/weekly routine that nurtures your faith, such as reading uplifting words by people who inspire you or engaging in meditation.

## 3. Be Kind to Yourself

While striving to get better, we are often our own worst critics. Faith takes a self-trust that can thrive only in the presence of patience and benevolence. The next time you start criticizing yourself, ask: "Would I choose these same words to criticize my partner or best friend?" If the answer is no, then don't use those words to criticize yourself.

Rewire your mind to choose more positive, uplifting words that will motivate you to do better instead of taking the wind out of your sails. Call in the strongest parts of you and let them be your guide as you nurture the parts that need more work. Call in the kind spirit in you who says, "Wait a minute—don't be so tough on yourself." Recognize where you're strong and let that help you tackle your weaknesses.

Here are some specific tips:

- **Write a letter to yourself.** Try writing a letter to yourself as though you're writing to a warm, loving friend. Read it whenever you're struggling to remember to treat yourself well.

- **Do the positive self-talk mirror exercise.** Every day, face a mirror and repeat three positive, supportive affirmations to yourself.

- **Forgive the cringe.** We all have moments we'd rather forget, ones that pop up and make us cringe when we're feeling down. Make a point to embrace the person you were then, thank yourself for the growth and evolution, and let the criticism fade away. Move on and have grace for your past self.

## 4. Listen to Your Intuition

Intuition is often described as inner wisdom or a gut feeling. It's a powerful tool in cultivating faith because it draws us closer to some level of knowledge that transcends reason.

To hear what's in your heart, slow down often and listen. You can do this through meditation, deep breathing, or even just being silent for a few minutes a day. With time, you will get a better understanding of your own voice and be able to lean into your gut feeling. If you've got a journal, jot down your intuitive experiences and what happens next. A pattern will emerge over time, and your recognition of it will help you build confidence in your own intuition.

Remember that you don't have to take your gut feelings at face value. In many cases, the best action is simply to sit with them and let your faith and intuition lead you to the right moment of action.

Make the time to quiet your mind so you can hear what your intuition is telling you. Have faith in your gut feeling and listen to what it's saying. You don't have to respond to everything immediately—in fact, it's often better to take time to thoroughly think things through before you act.

Here are some specific tips:

- **Do an intuition check-in.** Give yourself five minutes of quiet time each day to listen to your intuition. Ask yourself a question that's been on your mind and take note of what you hear.

- **Use your intuition in decision-making.** Make small, low-stake choices based on your intuition rather than your reason. Record the results.

- **Scan your body for intuitive signs.** Do a body scan meditation; observing bodily feelings you feel could be intuitive signals.

## 5. Practice Being Grounded

Faith is essential in challenging times, and I know from personal experience that these are some very challenging times we're living in today. Grounding exercises can make you feel more connected to yourself and the world around you while encouraging your faith. Try a grounding ritual every day. This might be as simple as standing on the ground barefoot or taking a few deep breaths and contemplating how connected you are to the earth. Take this opportunity to affirm that you're still believing in and trusting the process.

With grounding, you might find that you are able to keep faith in times of uncertainty and hardship. Visualize roots under your feet sinking into the ground and anchoring you, allowing you to consciously dial into your faith and trust in yourself and your guiding force.

Here are some specific tips:

- **Do an earth-connection ritual.** Stand for five to ten minutes a day on the earth, barefoot, as you imagine roots sprouting out of your feet and affirming your body's alignment with the ground.

- **Try a grounding conduit.** Select a grounding conduit (for example, a special stone or crystal) to carry with you—in a pocket, handbag, or backpack. Hold it when you want to feel grounded and connected to your faith. Different kinds of rocks and crystals are believed to have different properties, so experiment until you find the right ones for you.

- **Engage in faith-grounding breathwork.** Do a daily breathing practice in which you take a breath of faith and grounding from the earth and breathe out anxiety and self-doubt.

## 6. Use Faith to Process Your Moods and Emotions

I once heard someone refer to feelings of self-doubt as visitors who are just passing through. When things feel difficult, trust that the feeling is passing through—it's not permanent. We all live in an emotionally messy world, in which happy, sad, angry, and afraid feelings battle for control. Faith can be tremendously effective in working through these feelings, maintaining balance in the midst of high-level emotional states.

As a negative feeling strikes, don't question it. Instead, appeal to your faith to remind you that this sensation is temporary and will eventually pass. You could repeat the mantra "This too shall pass" or "I believe in my emotional tides—they are ever-changing from moment to moment, day to day." Faith helps you to let your feelings come through, and that will make you emotionally more resilient and calmer.

Here are some specific tips:

- **Let go.** As much as resilience is associated with grind culture, sometimes it's also about letting go and seeing what unfolds. Sometimes, faith is believing that what you need is right in front of you and if you ease up, let go, and pull back, it can be revealed more clearly.

- **Use faith anchor imagery.** Create a mental image of your belief (a mighty oak tree, a lighthouse that has withstood storm after storm for centuries). Consider picturing this mooring when you're feeling disorganized or down.

- **Check in with an emotional climate report.** Begin every day with a mindfulness exercise based on your current emotions and set an intention to listen with confidence to the reality of your situation—good, bad, or somewhere in between.

## 7. Help Others

Faith flourishes in community. Connecting with others, sharing experiences, and offering support are at the core of many faiths. We gain such relationships by supporting others' faith and becoming a source of strength and inspiration for ourselves. You confirm your own faith by doing something for others. With helping hands, you put your trust in action; you show faith through the virtues of kindness and understanding.

Be on the lookout for community projects you can get involved in. You might do this by volunteering, taking part in a community-based organization or just gathering together friends and neighbors for a picnic, cookout, or block party. When you make these connections with others, notice how they help you develop faith and strength in yourself.

As a reminder, when we are in service to others, we tend to help ourselves. Service can rekindle faith in the humanity of people and in our own goodness. Making the connections and building fellowship and community are cornerstones of faith and connection that allow you to build resilience through shared experiences and outcomes.

Here are some specific tips:

- **Engage in random acts of kindness.** Each day, make it a point to do one random act of kindness and consider how it makes you more hopeful about the human race.

- **Build a faith-sharing circle.** Plan or participate in an ongoing gathering where believers share their faith journeys and pray for one another. Of course, churches, synagogues, mosques, temples, and other houses of worship are perfect places for sharing your faith journey with others.

- **Create skill-faith bonds.** Find your gift or talent, then leverage it for others, in the process cementing the link between your talents and your faith.

## Conclusion

Cultivating faith is not a destination but an ongoing journey. It's a process of continual growth, self-discovery, and renewal. As you incorporate faith into your life—embracing it, giving yourself time and space, practicing self-kindness, listening to your intuition, grounding yourself, processing emotions, and building community—you'll likely find your faith deepening and your resilience growing.

Remember that faith is deeply personal. What works for

you might not work for someone else. Be patient with yourself as you explore different practices and find what resonates with you. Trust in the process, just as you're learning to trust in yourself and the greater forces at work in your life.

As you continue on this journey, you may find that your faith becomes a wellspring of strength, guiding you through life's challenges and celebrating its joys. It's a powerful tool for growth, one that can transform not only your own life but also the lives of those around you.

Embrace the journey of faith with all its twists and turns. Trust in yourself, in the process, and in the incredible potential for growth that lies within you. Your faith, cultivated with care and intention, can become an unshakeable foundation for a life of purpose, resilience, and joy.

## Bonus: Unique Perspectives on Faith

As a former divinity school student, I've had the privilege of meeting and working with faith leaders across the spectrum. I reached out to a small handful of these people for their stream-of-consciousness views on faith, and here are some of the replies I received.

### From my dear friend H. Scott Matheney, Chaplin and Dean of Religious Life at Elmhurst College:

Faith as storytelling, faith as spoken word, faith as beloved community. How do you find that community that accepts you? Affirms you? Carries you in your deepest moments like loss? Faith as the act of centering into holiness. Transcendence perspective. Faith that frames, informs in worship. The singing faith: think concerts, think solos that stir the soul. Think singing faith that sustains in times of death, singing faith that brings joy beyond imagination. Think of faith seeking understanding. Faith that learns and discovers. Faith that critiques, challenges expectations—resilience that speaks to faith that learns and discovers. Studies that liberate. Faith as building, resilience is about building. Think family of faith, your family structures and the community of faith that builds resilience. Think faith that doubts, questioning everything, questioning self, questioning others. Doubts are given to nurture a deeper resilience, deeper resistance to the brokenness of life. Faith as embodiment: the body given to you, wholeness. Think of disembodying, brokenness, imagine embodiment as resilience, a faith that embodies wholeness. A faith that prays: think of psalms, prayers of all life cycles, so write a prayer! For yourself, for someone you love. Prayer as resilience, prayer as resistance, release, reform, reimagination. Hope is a discipline; faith is a discipline. A system of structures that cultivate relationships. Respect. Resistance. Rest. Restlessness. Resilience. To quote Howard Thurman "Don't ask what the world needs. Ask what makes you come alive. And go do it! Because what the world needs is people who have come alive!"

### From Rabbi Steven B. Jacobs:

The Jewish people have a long tradition of resilience that has helped them survive for thousands of years. We find it in both its spiritual and practical aspects. Yes, faith involves resilience regardless of one's beliefs. Our values are found in faith; if one is true to himself or herself, then one becomes resilient to the vagaries of life. The Five Books of Moses, the Torah, begins with light overcoming darkness, teaching [us] that we can resist the darkness and protect the holiness of life and light. This is how we can go on living in the face of daily challenges. Pain and tragedy can help us survive. As our nation faces the erosion of hard-won civil and human rights, we must never stop our desires for hope, which strengthens the ability to be resilient. As Rev. Jesse Jackson always and in all ways says, "Keep hope alive." From hatred and war, from trauma to trauma, we can heal. *In Man's Search for Meaning*, one the most profound books of our time, Viktor Frankl asserts, "We have the power to change our lives through resistance and suffering. We can survive. Through resistance we can not only survive, we can find a greater purpose and meaning to our lives." Lamell McMorris guides us on our journey from trials and suffering toward resilience, finding our power and capacity to recover.

CHAPTER 10

# The Time Is Now

In this book, I have made it a point to tell stories from my own personal life, along with those of close friends, work associates, and others I know. I did this to ensure that you can see for yourself that *anyone* can succeed by putting resilience habits to work in their lives. However, there are some exceptional stories of resilience that involve people who have faced tremendous odds and emerged victorious in the end—people I don't personally know but who are household names.

I think the story of Simone Biles's journey from the jaws of defeat at the 2020 Tokyo Olympics to her triumphant return in the 2024 Paris Olympics is one of the most inspiring. It's a story of resilience, mental fortitude, and unwavering dedication, and it shows what can happen when you refuse to allow a missed opportunity, failure, or defeat to become the final word in the story of your life.

Hopes were high for the U.S. women's gymnastics team at the 2020 Olympics, and much of those hopes rested firmly on the shoulders of gymnastics phenomenon, Simone Biles. Simone had won four gold medals at the 2016 Olympics—along with nineteen world championship gold medals in the run-up to the 2020 games—and she and the U.S. women's team were heavy favorites to sweep the top spots. However, the COVID-19 pandemic disrupted the schedule for the Tokyo Olympic Games, and they took place in July and August 2021 instead of during the summer of 2020.

Simone's challenges began soon after she arrived in Tokyo. Because of the pandemic, no spectators were allowed, including Simone's parents—her biggest fans and supporters. In the qualification rounds, Simone bounced off the floor during one of her tumbling passes, stepped out of bounds while she executed a vault, and stumbled while dismounting from the balance beam. While she qualified in first place for the final team competition, it was clear that Simone was not her usual self—she wasn't in world championship form.

As she explained on Instagram, "I truly do feel like I have the weight of the world on my shoulders at times. I know I brush it off and make it seem like pressure doesn't affect me but damn sometimes it's hard hahaha! The Olympics is no joke!"[1]

Simone really did have the weight of the world on her shoulders, or at least the weight of millions of American fans who expected her to bring home the gold, no questions asked. But that wasn't to be for this Olympics.

After dialing down the difficulty of vaults she attempted during warm-ups for the first rotation of the team final, Simone withdrew from the team competition altogether—citing mental health issues—and subsequently withdrew from the finals of the individual all-round competition, the individual vault, uneven bars, and floor final. She decided to participate in the balance beam final and earned a bronze medal for her efforts—far below expectations.

Ultimately, Simone attributed her poor performance during the 2020 Olympic Games to something called the "twisties," which is a condition that causes gymnasts to lose their spatial awareness mid-air, making it difficult for them to perform complex routines. Of course, every one of Simone's routines was complex—and potentially dangerous. As Simone explained, "It doesn't feel comfortable. I have no idea where I am, but I'm twisting, praying I land on my feet. I felt like I was fighting my body and my mind to do these tricks."[2]

In addition to feeling like she failed her team and country, Simone felt like she had failed herself. She was slammed in the media as a "selfish psychopath," and "not a real athlete." Podcaster Charlie Kirk famously proclaimed, "We are raising a generation of weak people like Simone Biles. If she's got all these mental health problems: Don't show up." Then he went on to twist the knife he had plunged into her soul. "She's probably the greatest gymnast of all time. She's also very selfish, she's immature, and she's a shame to the country."[3]

The pressure on Simone in the wake of the 2020 Olympic Games was intense. "Oh, America hates me. The world is going to hate me," Simone explained in an interview. "I thought I was going to be banned from America. That's what they tell you: Don't come back if not gold. Gold or bust. Don't come back."[4] All this pressure might have crushed a lesser person, causing them to abandon their hopes and dreams and writing a sad ending to their story.

But Simone Biles refused to go down that road, and she drew from the deep well of resilience she had banked from the many successes she had previously experienced. She took a 732-day break from the sport that she loved so much, using the time to focus on her mental health as she gradually rebuilt her confidence and skills—methodically and deliberately. She simplified her routines and practiced in safer environments, such as foam pits, to regain her spatial awareness without the risk of injury. The good things she experienced during the course of her life and career in gymnastics helped her bounce back.

By 2024, Biles was ready to compete again. She placed first in the U.S. Gymnastics Trials, assuring her place on the Paris Olympics team. The way her routines at the trials wowed the judges was a testament to her practice and dedication. Despite falling off the balance beam on the second day of competition, she dominated the trials—finishing five points ahead of Sunisa Lee, the second-place finisher.

At the 2024 Paris Olympics, Biles returned with a vengeance against the twisties. She was focused and calm in her mind. Her routines were a mix of her trademark high-difficulty elements and brand-new moves. She led her team to a gold medal performance in the team all-around, won gold in the individual all-around and vault, and silver in the floor exercise—four medals in all.

Her multiple victories in Paris weren't just redemption for all the mental pain and anguish she suffered in the wake of the 2020 games; they were proof positive of the remarkable depth of the resilience she had accumulated as a result of her earlier victories. Simone Biles has once again inspired millions, proving that with a positive frame of mind, support, and determination, even the most daunting challenges can be overcome. Her journey from Tokyo to Paris is a testament to her resilience, illustrating that true greatness lies not just in winning medals but in the courage to face and overcome adversity.

While there is much to learn from Simone's example, I personally think these words—part of an interview she gave before the start of the 2024 Olympics—really get to the heart of what makes Simone Biles the greatest gymnast of all time: "I wanted to quit like 500,000 times and I would have if it weren't for my people. I knew it would be a long journey, but to me, it wasn't done. I'm going for another Olympic run, I never thought I'd be at this phase still doing it and I feel very grateful; I get to write my own ending."[5]

## Dig a Deep Well of Resilience

Being resilient for the long term, especially when we're under sustained pressure and stress—regardless of whether we're responding to opportunities or challenges—requires a multifaceted strategy. It involves filling a deep well of resilience during the good times, along with having a strong support system, practicing self-care, and learning to deal with all the change swirling around us in these challenging times.

While this book contains a proven set of rules and habits to unlock resilience, it also offers pathways—which are a bit more of a choose-your-own-adventure strategy—because people are unique and not everyone responds to strategies or motivations the same way. So, whether you're a code cracker or a path seeker, I hope you've found the methodologies in this book helpful, and I hope you'll continue to refer back to the frameworks put forth here as you determine what works for you when you face the inevitable life stages and challenges.

Building resilience is a lifelong journey! Some days it might require having gratitude for where you are (or aren't!). Some days it might be about asking more clearly for what you need. Some days it might be about asking yourself to push harder or further, which may require a shot of self-affirmation, kindness, and care—remembering that you're doing enough, you're doing great—to let out a big laugh and shine. All of these are forms of resilience, and all of these strategies are right here in these pages, so I hope this book becomes something you return to over and over again.

I'm again reminded of the devastation wreaked by Hurricane Helene and the stories of resilience—on an individual and community level—that were filling the pages of the news, social media accounts, and casual conversations among friends. Looking at this storm on a macro level brings the importance of resilience to mind in so many ways—certainly for individuals, but also for communities, for municipalities, for employers, for the faith community, and others. To survive a storm of that magnitude and to prepare for another, resilience must be incorporated in every step of the process.

As I look ahead to the future, I think about what resilient employers and companies that are able to weather the unexpected look like. I think about what they need to do when times are steady to prepare for the unknown. How do they strengthen and protect their workforces to fortify themselves during major events? We all saw the supply chain breakdown during COVID-19—who can forget driving all over town hunting for a pack of toilet paper? What have we learned about resilience—and what can companies do now to employ basic tactics to do better in the future?

In this book, I have laid out the key habits and pathways for building and maintaining resilience—what it takes to dig a deep well and fill it with an ever-growing supply of resilience that will sustain you through the inevitable ups and downs of life. Here are some of the most powerfully effective strategies I have found for putting these habits to work in your life right now:

## 1. Approach Challenges with a Growth Mindset

View challenges as opportunities to enhance your skill set. Be willing to learn—the moment we stop learning is the moment we stop growing. Seek out ways to learn from others—we are social creatures, and as such, we can all benefit from and learn from one another.

Instead of seeing the challenges in your life as barriers, look at them as opportunities for personal and professional growth. Each challenge is a learning opportunity, an opportunity to evolve and advance your talents. Remember, learning happens all the time. When you are no longer learning, you have stopped growing (and some would argue, you've stopped living).

Find coaches, coworkers, and friends to mentor and support you. We are sociable animals, and a huge part of personal and career development is learning from other humans—those we know and those we don't or who are new to us. Learning things by seeing others and exploring with them is a tremendously valuable experience.

In addition, develop an openness to unfamiliar experiences and concepts. Be willing to try new things, break barriers, and see difficulties as learning curves. With a growth mindset, you'll gain the strength and flexibility to face any challenge.

## 2. Nurture Relationships

Maintaining contact with coworkers, family, friends, neighbors, and others is important to our happiness. Be open about things that have gone well or poorly in your career, business, and life—doing so can help you heal, alleviate the pressure, and feel part of something more. It's possible to find resilience in good relationships.

Spend quality time and stay in touch with your family and friends—sharing the good times and the bad. Actively plan to get out of the house and be in the presence of others; talk with and provide emotional reassurance for one another. Recall that effective relationships depend on trust, open communication, and respect. Make the effort to build and nurture all of these.

### 3. Practice Self-Care

Overcoming obstacles and taking advantage of opportunities as they arise require being physically and mentally healthy. When you practice self-care through regular exercise, a balanced diet, and proper sleep, you'll be more energetic, happier, and more cognitively capable.

Also take time for your favorite things. Hobbies and interests can help you unwind, reduce stress, and have a positive attitude. For me, a day on the golf course with business associates or friends is one of my favorite things. It's a win-win situation—we get to relax, unwind, and have fun while building our relationships. Keep in mind that when you take care of yourself—when you make yourself a priority—you are not being selfish. You are filling your well of resilience.

### 4. Make Things Realistic

When you set goals, divide big challenges into smaller tasks so you don't get overwhelmed; have a sense of accomplishment as you tick them off your to-do list. If something feels impossible, take smaller steps to accomplish the goal—this can help you feel good about your progress as you get closer to your goal, motivating you to keep moving forward.

In addition, be patient with yourself if you need to put aside your task for a while as you deal with other priorities in your work or life. You can take time off or reroute your itinerary as necessary. Just make sure you stay on track with your overall goal and celebrate the progress you make along the way.

Finally, avoid the temptation to overcomplicate things. Go a little slower and recognize progress, not perfection. You will be motivated and won't burn the bridges when you make your objectives realistic and achievable.

## 5. Practice Mindfulness

Mindfulness is the act of attending in the moment without judgment. Practices such as meditation and journaling help to balance your feelings, alleviate your stress, and know yourself better. If you are mindful about being in the here and now, you will feel calmer and peaceful.

In addition to meditation and journaling, try mindfulness practices such as deep breathing, body scans, and conscious eating. These practices and others like them will help you increase your sense of being present in your world.

## 6. Get Some Help

When emotions get to be too much—which all of us experience from time to time—reach out to a therapist or counselor to work through feelings and develop coping mechanisms. These people are experts who can give you guidance, assistance, and resources to help you reduce stress and feel better about yourself. Remember, seeking help is a show of power, not weakness, and being vulnerable is a key habit in your resilience code. Speak with a mental health professional to build resilient coping skills.

Don't forget to find a support group. Being able to find like-minded people going through the same experiences as you are is tremendously helpful.

## 7. Facilitate Flexibility

Foster flexibility by being open to change and adapting plans in response to changing circumstances. Facilitate flexible thinking so your thinking processes can adjust to evolving environments.

The world is changing around us faster than ever before. Making yourself flexible is being willing to adjust and change your plans as the conditions change. If you adopt a pliable attitude, you can face problems easier and with greater strength.

Learn to be agile and think in a variety of different ways. Allow yourself to think outside of the box, question your beliefs, and change your mindset as you go. This talent can be invaluable in our ever-evolving world.

In addition, learn to problem-solve and make choices. As you learn to master these strategies, you'll have a better chance of facing unexpected situations and being creative as you work out solutions.

## 8. Take Part in Meaningful Activities

Doing things that bring you happiness and meaning can really make a difference for your well-being. Whether it's volunteering, having a passion for something, or even just going out and taking a walk through the neighborhood with your partner or family member, whatever you do in a meaningful way will connect you with others, take the pressure off, and bring you happiness.

You have to make time for things you truly enjoy, and when you do, you'll feel closer to yourself and to the world. Do things to have fun and be purposeful for your own well-being.

## 9. Think About Your Experiences

Looking back on your experiences with challenging situations can serve as a source of valuable insights and a boost to your self-esteem. Having awareness about your gifts and strengths allows you to believe more in yourself and your ability to move through the challenges that come your way.

Think often about how you handled past stressful events and succeeded in the process. This will help you realize that you can take the same course of action—or adjust it to your current circumstances—and succeed again. Don't forget that there's always room for improvement. Having a positive attitude, taking care of yourself, and having someone support you when you need it will make you stronger and provide you with the resilience you need to face the difficult events in life.

These strategies—and the many others we explored in the previous chapters—can help anyone build and maintain a deep well of resilience and navigate both opportunities and challenges over the long term.

## Write Your Own Ending

*Resilience* is a great word—it conjures up strength, invincibility, success, power. But it also brings up fear of failure, vulnerability, insecurity, inadequacy—that little voice in your mind asking, "What if I'm not resilient? What happens when it all falls apart and there's nothing left to do?"

I want to tell you that all of these feelings are OK and remind you that resilience is a muscle that needs to be strengthened. It's OK to worry about not meeting your goals, and it's OK to be afraid of even setting them because you're afraid you'll fall short. Resilience, and the habits that help you create and replenish it, are all part of this process!

It doesn't happen overnight, and building this muscle is not without setbacks. In fact, the setbacks are part of the process. It's hard to see this all play out in real time, but the setbacks—and the way you either bounce back from them or don't—will determine your success in the long run.

I can think of friends who, in their fifties, found themselves starting over from scratch after losing a job they'd had for twenty-five years or a marriage they'd known nothing other than. These are tough challenges—being spun out into a world with the only safety net you've ever known suddenly being cut from beneath you.

Unexpected challenges with health, relationships, careers—these are not just stories on a page but occurrences that can and will happen to all of us. And this is where your resilience habits come in. You've heard this before, but you are stronger than you think.

We humans are hardwired for survival, and it's our job to employ every cell in our bodies to be resilient, build resilience, practice resilience, and overcome the worst of what's in front of us.

Don't allow a missed opportunity, failure, or defeat to become the final word in the story of your life. Remember, it's you who writes the ending.

Yes, it's daunting. Yes, getting fired, getting divorced, losing a significant loved one, or confronting unexpected health issues—these are all really, really tough crossroads in life, and they're places that feel lonely, desperate, and scary. But remember that coming back from these challenges is a process—and building resilience is key.

If you work at it, it won't let you down.

If you commit to it, it will build you up.

It might happen quickly, or it might take some time, but this I promise you: The outcome is worth the effort.

# How Phase 2 Can Help Your Business and Community

**W**hat is resilience in business? It's your ability to thrive in a world filled with change, it's how quickly your systems return to normal operations after a shock, and it's the capability and capacity of your business to be agile and adapt over time. It's knowing what the plan is when a disruption occurs and how long you have to survive. It's preparedness, it's knowing the landscape, and it's your ability to work from a place of strength, no matter what the circumstances may be.

Today's business environment is complex and fast-changing —more than ever before. From social media to digital misinformation, there's no telling when the next crisis will occur or where it will come from. At the same time, there's no telling when your next great idea will lead to sudden and explosive growth. No matter which end of the spectrum your business is located on in any given day, resilience is the backbone of how well your business will adapt to change when it arrives.

My own business, Phase 2 Consulting, has incorporated business resilience into its workstreams—working with executives, founders, and business leaders on key components of organizational management to build and incorporate resilience at every turn, including the following:

- Being resilient in unpredictable social and political times

- Building and maintaining a resilient workforce

- Communicating across sectors within organizations to align internal departments on overlapping workflows

- Communicating to peers—employing resilience to show up in their industry

- Being embedded in communities to build community resilience

- Being prepared to respond to any crisis, be it environmental, PR-related, or the economy

- Using resilience to operate under pressure

- Using resilience to operate in a polarized or politically deadlocked environment

In addition, we work with cities, towns, and communities to ensure they are prepared to get through a major weather event or other disaster. We supply answers to key questions such as these:

- How can the basic tenets of resilience be better incorporated into city planning?

- What role does community resilience play in planning?

- What can communities do to increase resilience in times when people are increasingly online and less likely to know their neighbors in real life (IRL)?

- How can community institutions work to reengage neighbors to work together to build resilience?

We work with our clients to consider the following:

- Designing buildings for resilience using sustainable architecture

- Innovative stormwater management practices

- Community embeddedness for disaster response

- Community education on resilience and disaster preparedness

- Retrofitting buildings using environmentally resilient methods

- Zoning and code changes

- Communication changes that meet people where they are and understand community needs

- Mapping at-risk and vulnerable populations for disaster preparedness

Remember, the need for resilience is constant, and it's all around us—in everything we do. There's resilience needed in finance, resilience needed in energy, resilience needed in politics, resilience needed in medicine, resilience needed in academia, resilience needed in the arts, resilience needed in technology, and—especially given my passions and previous work and life's journey—resilience needed in building and sustaining communities.

These are just some of the challenges that lie ahead, and as someone who is on this journey personally, it is my hope that you begin to consider how what you've learned in this book can spill over into your job, your community, and the world at large. Know that we're here to support your journey every step of the way.

# Acknowledgments

I would like to extend my heartfelt thanks to Peter Economy and Cyd McKenna for being patient and remarkable collaborators throughout this journey. Your dedication and hard work were instrumental in bringing this manuscript to life.

I am also deeply grateful to the incredible team at Greenleaf. Your support as partners has made this historic effort a reality, and I will always cherish this milestone moment in my life.

To my dear friend and brother, Rev. Al Sharpton, it has been an honor to walk alongside you in the pursuit of justice and equality for all. Thank you for your honest and inspiring foreword, setting the tone for our continued journey toward resilience.

I want to acknowledge the invaluable sacrifice of time and insights from friends and loved ones who reviewed early drafts, participated in interviews, or simply listened to my thoughts on this project. A special thank you to Mike Ross, Elizabeth Thomas, Kent Matlock, and Ray Anderson for sharing your truths regarding my story.

Dr. Larry Rice, Dr. Manica Ramos, and Dr. J.D. LaRock, your critiques provided clarity and depth that were essential to my writing. I also appreciate David Kohler, Chris Womack,

Marc Morial, Michelle Morial, Dorri McWhorter, Jordyn Hudson, LaReina Shaw, Kathy Behrens, Larry Kopp, Dawn Schneider, and Joe Nocera for your honest feedback—thank you for telling me what I needed to hear, even when it wasn't what I wanted to hear.

To all of you, I cannot express my gratitude enough. Your support has been invaluable on this journey.

# Notes

## Introduction

1. Ron Chepesiuk, *Black Gangsters of Chicago* (Barricade Books, 2007), 125.

2. Chepesiuk, *Black Gangsters of Chicago*, 126.

3. James Alan McPherson, "Chicago's Blackstone Rangers (Part I)," *The Atlantic*, May 1969, https://www.theatlantic.com/magazine/archive/1969/05/chicagos-blackstone-rangers-i/305741/.

## Chapter 1

1. Holly Hinton, "Psychologist Ann Masten Talks about Resilience During 2024 Grawemeyer Award Lecture," *UofL News*, April 25, 2024, https://www.uoflnews.com/section/arts-and-humanities/psychologist-ann-masten-talks-about-resilience-during-2024-grawemeyer-award-lecture/.

2. Ann S. Masten and Auke Tellegen, "Resilience in Developmental Psychopathology: Contributions of the Project Competence Longitudinal Study," *Developmental Psychopathology* 24, no. 2 (May 2012), https://pubmed.ncbi.nlm.nih.gov/22559118/.

3. Julie Tremaine, "All About Simone Biles' Parents, Ronald and Nellie Biles," *People*, August 5, 2024, https://people.com/sports/all-about-ronald-nellie-biles-simone-biles-parents/.

4. Sarah Fleishman, "Airbnb, VRBO and Short-Term Rentals One of Few Winners in the COVID-Crippled Travel Industry," SensorTower, April 2021, https://sensortower.com/blog/airbnb-vrbo-and-short-term-rentals-one-of-few-winners-in-the-covid-crippled-travel-industry.

5. "Supply Chain Resiliency: Three Companies with Resilient Supply Chains Setting the Example," John Carroll University, April 27, 2022, https://blog.jcu.edu/2022/04/27/companies-with-supply-chain-resilience/.

## Chapter 2

1. "Hurricane Helene: Over 220 Dead as Some Communities Struggle to Get Basic Supplies," *NBC News*, October 4, 2024, https://www.nbcnews.com/news/weather/live-blog/hurricane-helene-live-updates-rcna173973.

2. Gail Ironson, Emily Hylton, and Rachel Verhagen, "A New Attitude Towards Treatment Measure Predicts Survival Over 17 Years," *Journal of General Internal Medicine*, August 2022, https://www.ncbi.nlm.nih.gov/pmc/articles/PMC9360262/.

3. Lewina Lee, Peter James, Emily Zevon, and Laura Kubzansky, "Optimism Is Associated with Exceptional Longevity in 2 Epidemiologic Cohorts of Men and Women," *PNAS*, August 26, 2019, https://www.pnas.org/doi/10.1073/pnas.1900712116.

4. Jeff Aguy, "Empowering Change: Demitrea Kelley's Fight for Sickle Cell Awareness and Community Resilience," LinkedIn, September 3, 2024, https://www.linkedin.com/pulse/empowering-change-demitrea-kelleys-fight-sickle-cell-awareness-aguy-j5esc/.

## Chapter 3

1. Shannon, "DC Mythbusting: 'Lobbyist' Coined at Willard Hotel," We Love DC, June 9, 2009, https://www.welovedc.com/2009/06/09/dc-mythbusting-lobbyist-coined-at-willard-hotel/.

2. Tania Barney, "How Much Time Do You Lose to Distractions?" Workplace Events, n.d., https://workplaceevents.co/how-much-time-do-you-lose-to-distractions/.

## Chapter 4

1. Melissa De Witte, "50 Years on, Mark Granovetter's 'The Strength of Weak Ties' Is Stronger Than Ever," *Stanford Report*, July 24, 2023, https://news.stanford.edu/stories/2023/07/strength-weak-ties.

## Chapter 5

1. Brené Brown, "The Power of Vulnerability," TEDxHouston, June 2010, https://www.ted.com/talks/brene_brown_the_power_of_vulnerability.

## Chapter 8

1. Angela Duckworth, *Grit: The Power of Passion and Perseverance* (New York: Scribner, 2016).

2. Mark Granovetter, "The Strength of Weak Ties," *American Journal of Sociology* 78, no. 6 (May 1973): 1360–1380.

3. Melissa De Witte, "50 years on, Mark Granovetter's 'The Strength of Weak Ties' is Stronger Than Ever," *Stanford Report*, July 24, 2023, https://news.stanford.edu/stories/2023/07/strength-weak-ties.

## Chapter 9

1. Jeffrey Jones, "In U.S., 47% Identify as Religious, 33% as Spiritual," Gallup, September 22, 2023, https://news.gallup.com/poll/511133/identify-religious-spiritual.aspx.

2. Hebrews 11:1, King James Version (KJV).

3. Samuel DeWitt Proctor, *The Substance of Things Hoped for: A Memoir of African-American Faith* (New York: Putnam Adult, 1996).

## Chapter 10

1. Simone Biles, "Prelims now to prepare for finals," Instagram, July 25, 2021, https://www.instagram.com/p/CRxsq_kBZrP/.

2. Max Molski, "What Are the Twisties? How Simone Biles Bounced Back from the Gymnastics Phenomenon," *5NBCDFW*, June 28, 2024, https://www.nbcdfw.com/paris-2024-summer-olympics/twisties-explained-simone-biles-gymnastics-olympics/3579756/.

3. Brenley Goertzen, "Charlie Kirk, Piers Morgan Slam Simone Biles as a 'Selfish Sociopath' and 'Shame to the Country,'" *Salon*, July 28, 2021, https://www.salon.com/2021/07/28/charlie-kirk-piers-morgan-slam-simone-biles-shes-a-selfish-sociopath-shame-to-the-country/.

4. Emma Hruby, "Simone Biles Talks Tokyo Olympics Fallout in New Interview," *Just Women's Sports*, April 18, 2024, https://justwomenssports.com/reads/simone-biles-tokyo-olympics-banned-america-gymnastics/.

5. Nischal Schwager-Patel, "'I Feel Very Grateful I Get to Write My Own Ending': Simone Biles Discusses Spectacular Olympic Comeback in New Documentary," *Olympics*, June 20, 2024, https://olympics.com/en/news/simone-biles-spectacular-olympic-comeback-new-documentary.

# About the Author

**Dr. Lamell McMorris** grew up in the South Side of Chicago and went on to find phenomenal success as an entrepreneur, a D.C.-policymaker, a consultant in the financial and professional sports arenas, a civil and human rights advocate, as well as in a Fortune 300 securities firm.

Dr. Lamell McMorris is the founder and CEO of the Washington, D.C–based company Phase 2 Consulting. Dr. McMorris offers strategic insight and external affairs services to some of the nation's leading decision-makers in the private, public, and nonprofit sectors. Additionally, he manages an in-house team of experienced government and public relations professionals and lawyers, offering a multitude of services to clients in a wide range of disciplines and specialty areas.

In recent years, through Perennial Sports, Dr. McMorris led a premier, full-service sports agency representing NFL and NBA players and personalities. Collectively, its agents signed multiple first-round picks and negotiated several multimillion-dollar contracts.

Dr. McMorris is an active and effective fundraiser. As a lifelong advocate of civil, economic, and human rights, Dr.

McMorris serves as a member of numerous nonprofit and college boards. He volunteers his time with several youth-focused and mentoring organizations. He is frequently recognized for his entrepreneurial leadership and pragmatic, high-impact approach to effective advocacy, and he is often invited to speak at a wide range of conferences and events. Dr. McMorris holds a bachelor of arts in religion and society from Morehouse College, a master of divinity in social ethics and public policy from Princeton Theological Seminary, and a doctorate in law and policy from Northeastern University.